American Sportscars

GALLERY BOOKS
An imprint of W.H. Smith Publishers Inc.
112 Madison Avenue
New York, New York 10016

A SURVEY OF THE CLASSIC MARQUES

RICHARD NICHOLS

A QUINTET BOOK
produced for
GALLERY BOOKS
An imprint of W. H. Smith Publishers Inc.
112 Madison Avenue
New York, New York 10016

ISBN 0-8317-1453-0

This book was designed and produced by
Quintet Publishing Limited
6 Blundell Street
London N7 9BH

Art Director: Peter Bridgewater
Designer: Stuart Walden
Editors: Shaun Barrington, Patricia Bayer

Typeset in Great Britain by
Central Southern Typesetters, Eastbourne
Manufactured in Hong Kong by
Regent Publishing Services Limited
Printed in Hong Hong by
South Sea International Press Ltd.,

CONTENTS

The strangest thing about the automobile is that the novelty still hasn't worn off. More than 100 years after the first motor cars spluttered into life the romance of powered motion, the lure of individual mobility and the freedom it represents, is as strong as ever – probably stronger.

And, aside from a decade of gloom and despondency in the 1970s, throughout that 100 years the car has been more than a means of transport; it has been a method of self-expression, a form of vanity, an alter ego and, if you go to the limit with theories, a Freudian glimpse into the mind of its owner.

Amid all the philosophizing – and there's been plenty of it – there is more than a little hard truth. Certainly a car is an expression of status, prestige and aspiration; people judge their fellow man by appearance, by clothing and accessories and by the type of car he or she drives. And few cars are able to inspire the same emotions as the sports car. We all make similar assumptions about sports cars, and the people who drive them. They seem to have different priorities, different values, a more exciting approach to life – and a lot more fun.

To begin with, of course, there was no such thing as a sports car. All cars were fundamentally the same, and their prime concern was to get from A to B without too many hold-ups, difficulties or breakdowns. In order to demonstrate that sort of reliability, the early manufacturers used their cars on endurance runs, proving that they could get from one place to another without a problem, and faster than the horse they were hoping to replace. Within a short space of time the competitive instinct of the human race was aroused, and those proving runs became endurance trials and then races.

After a while the question was not so much one of survival, but of speed. Everyone knew the car could get from A to B. What interested them was – how quickly?

That question is still the major preoccupation of car enthusiasts and owners.

Even so, the evolution of the sports car was slow; early manufacturers entered their regular production cars for trials and races, rather than build specially for them, since that was the whole point. Later, they followed the styles set by carriage and coach makers, with a "family" body for the bulk of buyers but developing a more rakish body for the single-man-about-town who wished to enjoy life to the full. These gentleman's roadsters, as they were called, were the immediate precursors of the type of car that today takes many forms but which we still group under the generic heading of "sports car".

For many observers, Vauxhall's 1911 "Prince Henry" was the first car properly classified as a purpose-built sports car. Later European-built cars with a sporting flavor followed the established formula: low chassis frame, long hood, two seats and a short deck. For some reason the European manufacturers excelled in this field. Though the American industry was something of a late starter, its enormous industrial muscle and vast market potential soon meant that Detroit dominated the world in output, quality and style – in the area of family sedans, anyway. There seemed to be only a small demand for sporting cars, not enough for Detroit to find a profit in it, so it was left to small specialists to meet it.

Thus there sprang up a sort of two-pronged approach to the sports car; independent car makers supplied the sporting

engine and chassis and coach builders like Fisher, Le Baron, Fleetwood and so on supplied the ravishing full-fendered bodies to go on top. That was the expensive end of the market. The alternative was the enthusiast racer, who went the other way entirely, stripping his family car of bodywork to make it smaller, lighter, handier and, naturally, faster. Before long there were specialist firms which existed solely to meet the needs of that market.

So on the one hand came Mercer, probably the best-known example of the the Raceabout style, prompted by the specialist component makers, among whom was Erret Cord (who had supplied parts for cars like the Model T Speedsters) and the specialist engine-builders like Frontenac, who supplied the power.

And on the expensive side of the fence sat people like Packard, who made gentlemen's roadsters, and the real sports car builders like Stutz, Duesenberg and, later, Auburn and Cord. But the Depression, which hit the USA hard (Europe less so) more than halved the number of auto manufacturers in North America. Many of those which disappeared were the specialists, and many of the bigger makers who were willing to dabble in the sporting end of the market in the 1920s were forced to draw in their horns.

Packard began a downsizing program which effectively ended its participation in that sort of market and eventually closed the firm forever. The Auburn-Cord-Duesenberg empire of Erret Cord made some splendid, even outrageous, sports cars but folded in a fit of excess in the late 1930s. When the United States went to war in 1941, European makers like Jaguar, MG, Frazer-Nash, Morgan and so on had established a huge margin of expertise in sports car design and manufacture.

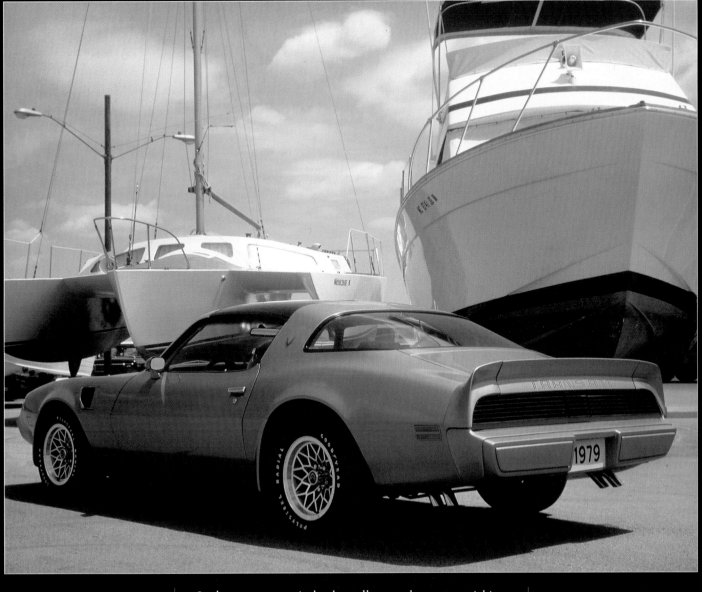

LEFT AND ABOVE LEFT *Edsel Ford's Lincoln Continental, the 1941 equivalent of the gentleman's roadster.*

ABOVE *Far more brash and overstated, the 1979 Firebird.*

In the postwar period, when all car makers were picking up the pieces gradually, most sports cars were, like family cars, built to pre-war designs. The only difference was that the homing GIs had driven and enjoyed the small two-seaters and the European car makers were faced with an "export or die" choice. A few went under, many exported, and a few famous names like Ferrari and Porsche joined in for the first time. It was in response to these cheap imports that a new wave of independent specialists sprang up all over the United States – Devin, Bocar, Reventlow, Scarab, Kaiser and Cunningham were a few, and their activities seem to have been the spur behind the Corvette and then the Thunderbird.

The attempts made by giant auto makers like GM and Ford to keep up with the expertise of the small specialists met with mixed results. Though the technology, the talent and the enthusiasm were all present it appears that the blue pencil of cost accountancy robbed too many projects of too many elements for the American sports car to have been competitive in world terms. All of which held true until the sixties, when it ceased to matter so much. That was because Pontiac, then the rest of Detroit, discovered the performance-orientated youth market

OVERLEAF *Born in 1964, the Mustang is still going strong today.*

OVERLEAF, RIGHT *Studebaker's last-ditch attempt at survival, the Corvette-based Avanti.*

and developed the musclecar especially for its rather unsophisticated tastes.

Suddenly the USA had its own breed of sports car, and the GTO, Road Runner, Challenger, Coronet and all the others were the hot-selling lines. In 1965 Ford launched the Mustang, a sort of American sports car compromise, and sparked off a second wave of performance cars with Camaro, Firebird, Javelin and Trans Am at its spearhead. All of that died away when the gas crisis arrived in the early 1970s. The performance market went quiet and only Corvette continued to carry the banner.

All through the musclecar era Corvette had quietly improved; better than ever by the late 1960s, it had seen off the brash upstarts from Shelby, outlasted the pretenders and clung determinedly to its title – American's only *real* sports car. When it was redesigned in the early eighties it joined the "supercar" league, leaving GM to contest the sports car market with much-

improved Camaro-Firebird models and its award-winning new Fiero. Without its 300hp-plus aluminum engine Fiero potential remains unresolved, although there was a time when it looked set to topple Corvette's crown and take over the kingdom entirely.

But outside of Corvette, say "sports car" and most Americans think either of a European import or – perhaps even more likely now – of Toyota Supra, Mazda RX-7 or the amazingly popular Nissan Z-car. Which is a shame: the heritage is there, the tradition is there and the profit is there.

Whether Ford will get the new Pantera off the ground remains to be seen. The news that Chrysler will follow the Shelby specials with a Lamborghini tie-up is certainly very promising. And Cadillac's beautiful Allanté demonstrates the potential that still exists. If Detroit put the same effort into low-volume specialist cars it does into family sedans, then American-built sports cars could be the best in the world.

1914
STUTZ
BEARCAT

PRODUCTION SPAN

1914–17
(and in revived form to the
present)

ENGINE

4-cyl in-line sidevalve
T-head

CAPACITY

6.5 litres/396ci

MAXIMUM POWER

60bhp @ 1500rpm

CHASSIS/SUSPENSION

Pressed steel frame with
tubular crossmembers,
forged front axle and three-
speed rear transaxle; semi-
elliptic leaf springs all round

BODY STYLE

2-seat open body with
monocle windshield

TOP SPEED

Not recorded

The first "real" car produced by Harry Stutz was also what many people accept as one of the USA's first "sports" cars. The American Underslung, as it was called, appeared in 1905, and it carried the chassis frame beneath the springs instead of the other way around, which was – and still is – the conventional approach. It was not the best solution to the handling problem, and Stutz continued his search for a better answer. It came in the shape of a low frame allowing high cornering speeds, and that was the vital advantage which the Stutz Black Hawk team had over the Bentleys at Le Mans.

Harry Stutz began his life in the auto industry as a racer, and he went on to build bigger and better race cars. By 1913 the company was building its own four- or six-cylinder engines. In 1913 a Stutz placed third at Indy, and in 1914 came what is now considered an all-time classic, the Stutz Bearcat. This 6.5-liter straight four developed about 60hp at 1500rpm, and it was this car that began the bitter rivalry between Stutz and Mercer owners which existed both on and off the track.

Squat, even ugly in appearance, the Bearcat was also something of a handful to drive – a combination of crude suspension, short wheelbase and plenty of power. The Raceabout certainly did handle better than the Stutz. But the Bearcat's power seemed to outweigh that completely; certainly Stutz won more races than Mercer.

Then in 1915 the Stutz racing team appeared. Known as the "White Squadron" because of their white livery and white racing coveralls, they were third, fourth and seventh at Indy that year, and won a number of other events during the season. And when a Bearcat owner complained, in a blaze of publicity, that Mercer's were faster and were beating him, Harry Stutz seized the opportunity to pull off a brilliant marketing coup.

There were few roads anywhere in America, but the Bearcat in question – dubbed a "lemon" by the press – was given to a racing driver to make a well-publicised attempt on the coast-to-coast record, held at the time by a cross-country motorcyclist. The drive created a legend which has lasted until the present time as an illegal event and is part of the folklore of American motoring. "Cannonball" Baker gave his name to the coast-to-coast crossing, making the trip in 11½ days. He set a record and the "lemon" behaved perfectly all the way.

Harry Stutz left his company in 1919, and a succession of rather staid sedan cars filled the following years, including the unsporting Safety Stutz. Then came the revival of the Black Hawk, a car close to the spirit of the original and based on the Stutz-built 198mph (317km/h) Land Speed Record car. That signaled a return to the racetrack and Stutz figured prominently in the 1928 24 hours at Le Mans.

The Stutz came close to ending the Bentley domination of the Sarthe circuit and almost put Stutz and the United States into the international winner's circle for the very first time. The honor eventually went to Ford and Shelby in 1966, but in 1928 only a lost gear ratio prevented an American victory, as "Babe" Barnato hung on to his lead and the Black Hawk limped in ahead of the other two 4.5-liter Bentleys.

The rumored 24 blown "specials" that were said to have been built for the 1930 event never appeared, at Le Mans or anywhere else. From then on it was downhill through the Depression, and the Stutz firm closed its doors in 1935.

PREVIOUS PAGE *Harry Stutz made his name with his squat, unattractive but powerful roadsters, like this 1919 Bearcat.*

TOP *Back on a racetrack after half a century, Harry Stutz and the White Squadron were the only American race cars to get close to a major international championship when they chased the Bentleys home at Le Mans in 1928. US ambitions had to wait until the 1-2-3-4 procession of Shelby GT40s put Ford in the winner's circle at Sarthe in 1966.*

ABOVE AND LEFT *Virgil Exner's design of the modern Stutz Blackhawk included a 1930s style radiator which echoed the Bearcat's, but that is about as close as the two machines get.*

ABOVE AND LEFT *Years after the death of Harry Stutz, his name is revived in the new Blackhawk, a real curiosity which gains little favor among purists, though it is beyond doubt an exceptional car, with its outlandishly sculptured body panels and gold plated interior.*

MERCER TYPE 35 RACEABOUT

PRODUCTION SPAN
1911–1919

ENGINE
4-cyl sidevalve T-head

CAPACITY
5 litres/305ci

MAXIMUM POWER
50bhp

CHASSIS/SUSPENSION
Pressed steel ladder,
semi-elliptic leaf springs all
round

BODY STYLE
Open two-seater
(windscreen added in 1919)

TOP SPEED
70mph

"There's nothing worser than a Mercer" was how Stutz owners used to greet the drivers of their deadliest rivals. Their unkind verse was a response to the Mercer owners' often-repeated saying, "You have to be nuts to drive a Stutz". From the very earliest days there was a rivalry between the two sets of owners, and it was in large part due to the scarcity of domestic-built sports cars and to the rough equality between the two.

Mercer definitely had it on looks. Lower and longer, it had a grace which stemmed from a chassis that was economical in weight and strength. In fact, the flexing that went on within it was an integral part of the suspension. Even so, most were raced cross-country at some time, and almost every surviving example has chassis repairs that could easily date right back to the year of manufacturer. But it worked, and it had a certain precision in its handling that made other cars – including the Stutz – seem clumsy by comparison.

Mercers came from Trenton, in Mercer County, New Jersey. The company was the result of a liaison between the Roeblings and Kusers, two affluent families who were indulging a personal liking for small, nimble cars with which to enjoy the fast-growing craze for auto racing. The Mercer was among the earliest of the sports car breed to be built anywhere in the world.

The first, the Model 30-C Speedster, was completed in 1909, and was an "assembled" car. Even in the pioneering days a factory and plant were too expensive for most people, and so would-be car makers bought components from outside suppliers and bolted them together in a unique design. Built in this way, the 1909 Speedster used a straight four by Beaver; Mercer stuck with this supplier for some time, allowing a mutual development that saw engine and car improve together. The more powerful Beaver L-head engine found a useful home

RIGHT *The Mercer Type 35 Raceabout offered only primitive weather protection. Dash and instrumentation (inset) were also exposed.*

BELOW *The 'stirrup' for the accelerator pedal is visible, and even from here you can see the left front wheel.*

in the heavier two-seater designed for Mercer by Erik Delling, a car guaranteed to be capable of 75mph (120km/h).

Then in 1911 came the Type 35 Raceabout. Designed by Finlay Robertson Porter, its four-cylinder T-head engine and a three-speed gearbox gave it a slightly lower top speed; with a four-speed that improved a little. The Raceabout was offered ready to race off the showroom floor, but the racers' modifications made it faster still. The engine was over-engineered and over-heavy; racers traditionally believe that any component that can't be broken in a race is too heavy. The belief seems to have begun with the Raceabout; most of its moving components (especially the flywheel) were ruthlessly machined down. Later still came another racing adage – that bigger is better – and the 300ci engine was simply replaced with a larger 450.

The 1911 Raceabout was not just some marketing oddity with a short production run: at a reasonable price of $2,250, it cut out a whole new market for itself and for its imitators. The Stutz Bearcat was to feed off the Mercer's success.

But there was little weight-saving to be found on the body. In fact there wasn't a great deal of bodywork to be found at all. There were no doors, for there was no real cockpit. The precious engine was fully enclosed, but the driver was left out in the open, with nothing more than a tiny "monocle" windshield. The driver's seat was on the right side of the car, and

bodywork was so basic that he could easily see the left front wheel. What this shows more than anything is that the Raceabout was designed and built for short, competitive outings, not for touring or socializing.

Calling it a sports car is misleading. It was a race car, and began to prove it by winning races over short distances at speeds well about 75mph (120km/h). It was driven by people like Spencer Wishart, Barney Oldfield, Eddie Pullen and Ralph de Palma in the years leading up to World War I. In 1913, Wishart took a racing type 35F – the smallest car in the race – to Indianapolis, and came second.

But it wasn't easy to drive; the gas pedal was outside the bodywork, and there was a brass stirrup for the driver's heel. The footbrake was famous for its almost total lack of effect, and drivers had to use the handbrake if they wanted to stop. Later versions, like the 1915 L-head Model 22-70, became more sophisticated, with luxuries like doors, a full-size windshield and even a self-starter. By this time Mercer had followed Ford; and adopted left-hand drive.

As the controlling families retired, Mercer was taken over by a Wall Street combine, which turned to the manufacture of discreet and genteel tourers. This was never successful for them; Mercer was in receivership by 1923 and closed by 1925. Of almost 5,000 cars built, fewer than 100 survive.

PACKARD TWIN SIX

PRODUCTION SPAN
1915–1923

ENGINE
60-degree V12, sohc sidevalve

CAPACITY
6950cc/424ci

MAXIMUM POWER
85bhp

CHASSIS/SUSPENSION
Pressed steel chassis frame, semi-elliptic leaf springs all round

BODY STYLE
Various

TOP SPEED
60–70mph approx

In 1898 James Packard bought a Winton car; they were a popular make but Packard thought he could do better. When he said as much to Alexander Winton, it was suggested he try it. Winton must have wished he'd held his tongue, for the first Packard appeared in 1899 and proved the point. It was much better, and Packards continued in production long after Winton had closed down. In fact Packard went on to better and better things, eventually becoming the transport of Presidents and one of the great names of the American auto industry.

Renowned for the manufacture of formal limousines, Packard built its cars in the classic era, when auto makers often (and sometimes only) supplied a rolling chassis with engine for their customers to "body" as they chose. In that respect, there may have been little difference between the chassis and running gear of the six-seat sedan and the four-seat gentleman's roadsters outside the bodywork. Consequently it is the bodywork which endows a car with its sporting flavor in many cases. In their heyday, Packard had its nameplate on some rakish-looking vehicles that were styled to be sport- and leisure-orientated rather than formal.

BELOW LEFT *The 'Super Eight' emblem*

The first single-cylinder Packard established a reputation for reliability and excellence; not for nothing did Cadillac have to beat Packard's reputation before it could claim to be "best". When a 12hp single-cylinder Model F (later known as "Old Pacific") crossed the USA from coast to coast, it gave Packard an even stronger reputation for reliability and imparted a somewhat sporting character to the marque. The journey had only ever been done once before – by a Winton – and Old Pacific finished it in 61 days, clipping two days off the record.

In 1904 Packard introduced its four-cylinder K-type race car. Called "The Gray Wolf", it set records at Daytona and came fourth in the first ever Vanderbilt Cup. Packard naturally used sporting achievements in his advertising, even though the concept of the purebred sports car had not arrived. The sportier models in the Packard line-up – such as the 1910 Thirty Thirty – were described in the literature as "Gentleman's Roadsters". That was mainly because all forms of motoring were still the preserve of the wealthy, and more and more "gentlemen" en-

joyed the competitive aspects of the new craze.

But that began to change as the automobile started to change the face of the world. As the car became more and more accessible, different styles began to develop. In 1915 Packard produced its Twin Six. It had V12 power, was well-made and good looking, still used the two-wheel braking sytem then in vogue, and became a well-liked boulevardier. Its success in the fashionable city streets gave Packard a distinct lever in an up-

LEFT *Emblems like this are illegal in most countries of the world today.*

ABOVE *1934 Packard V12 'Orello'.*

TOP RIGHT *Independent front suspension ensured a comfortable ride.*

market direction, and by the early 1920s Packards were *the* American car to own. Henry Leland's Lincoln was second choice, Cadillac was next and there were some exclusive (and raffish) models coming from the Rolls-Royce factory in Springfield, Massachusetts.

Packard turned its corporate back on the sporting cars, preferring instead to concentrate on the higher prices (and higher profits) which could be earned from larger cars. When the

Depression struck, Packard was hard hit, and turned to the manufacture of smaller and smaller cars in order to survive. Its eight- and six-cylinder cars were described as "dismal" by Packard traditionalists, even though the scheme met with some success. By 1937 production of the six- and eight-cylinder cars soared to over 100,000 units. But survival wasn't enough; the Packard reputation for superb hand-made sports cars "for gentlemen" – like the excellent Model 734 boat-tail Speedster of 1929-39 – was forever tarnished.

In 1931 Prince Eugene of Belgium had used two Packard Series Eights as personal transport for a trip across the Sahara desert, and that was the market Packard was aiming for once again. Throughout the 1930s the firm offered a range of V12 cars with some brilliant coachwork designs by Dietrich. And there were other good-looking classics, too, with coachwork from Rollston, Le Baron and, best of a highly creditable collection, the designs of Howard Darrin. Best of all his efforts was the convertible Darrin Victoria, based on the 120 chassis.

The war saved Packard from closure; the company built Rolls-Royce Merlin engines under license, and emerged into the 1950s still struggling to catch up with Cadillac and Lincoln. Once again it failed, and a measure of that failure came under the leadership of Jim Nance. He renounced Packard's illustrious past in an attempt to start over, but incredibly he directed that Packard's priceless archives be destroyed and the parts inventory that was keeping the older Packards on the road be sent to the junkyard.

If any single act spelled doom for Packard, then that was it. Two years later they merged with Studebaker, already in even worse financial trouble than Packard. A series of mediocre "lookalike" cars, which were often unkindly called "Packardbakers", more or less sealed its fate. Nance resigned when the combine was acquired by Curtiss-Wright as a humiliating tax loss. In 1958, with a total production run for the year below 3,000 units, Packard, once the most illustrious name in the industry, closed its doors forever.

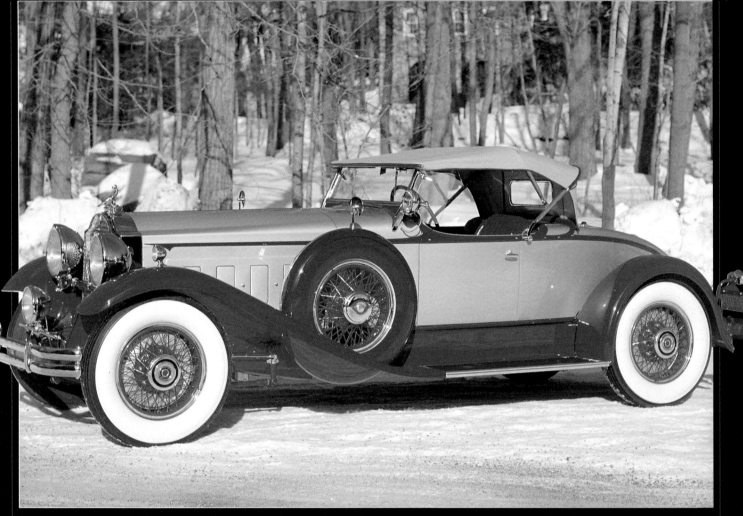

FORD MODEL T SPEEDSTER

PRODUCTION SPAN

Conversions based on
Model T Ford 1908–27

ENGINE

4-cyl in-line sidevalve

CAPACITY

2896cc/176ci

MAXIMUM POWER

20bhp

CHASSIS/SUSPENSION

Steel channel-section chassis
frame; transverse leaf
springs front and rear

BODY STYLE

Open two-seater

TOP SPEED

Various

It may seem strange, at first, to find the Model T described as a sports car, but such were its roots, and that is just one of the many roles it enjoyed in its long life. Until the Volkswagen Beetle came along, it was also the biggest-selling car in the world.

In 1906 Henry Ford unveiled his vision of the automobile's future, the Model T, a five-seater with a top speed of 40mph (64km/h), priced at $850. Its 2.9-liter four-cylinder engine introduced a number of new features and also used a number of "borrowed" ideas, like the Lanchester flywheel magneto. And it was unusual for the driver, too, with separate pedals for forward and reverse instead of a gear lever, a throttle that doubled as a brake (press to go, lift off to stop) and an advance/retard lever mounted on the steering wheel.

Its light steel frame flexed over rough surfaces, acting as a suspension element – its transverse leaf springs had no shock absorbers. The early cars were bodied in wood shaped over wooden struts, and only later was sheet metal used instead.

In order to attract attention and sales, Henry Ford had built his own reputation on the racetrack with cars like Arrow and 999, and it was inevitable that as the Model T became available in larger and larger quantities it too would find its way onto the racetrack. Stripped down, the early buckboard Ts raced on dirt ovals, the quarter-mile board tracks at county fairs, Pike's Peak, anywhere there was racing.

The first techniques were simply to remove all the bodywork except the hood and a cowl for the driver to crouch behind, in a bucket-type seat bolted to the chassis, and with the steering column dropped down to suit. Later on there were "after-market extras" for the race enthusiasts, things like grille shells which gave the then-tiny accessory market a boost into large-scale production. Indeed, many household names began life as small independents serving the needs of Model T owners with the luxuries missing from their basic Model T. Frontenac started a new trend altogether with a 16-valve conversion for the Model T engine.

The process blossomed, and soon you could buy whole Speedster bodies, full-fendered designs that clothed the skeletal buckboard racers. Within a short time there were

RIGHT *The Model T Speedster with typical stripped bodywork and 'monocle' windshield.*

BELOW RIGHT *Engine detail from the 1915 Speedster. Brass headlamps (far right) were non-standard by 1915.*

BELOW *The Model T as it came from the factory . . .*

special "sports" bodies available that were never meant to be used on a race track. Superbly crafted, painted and trimmed, they were the forerunners of the gentleman's roadster, itself the harbinger of the purpose-built sports car. As such, they incorporated all the visual styling cues that remained with the sports car right up to the full-width styling of postwar days – and that means the fifties.

Low chassis, brass radiator shell and huge brass lamps, small aero screen ahead of the driver and absolutely zero weather protection – it could be a description of an MG TD, an Auburn or a Bugatti from later years. But in this form the Model T, so earthily practical, had an elegance all its own.

During the Model T's incredible 19-year lifespan, in which production averaged almost a million cars each year, the Speedsters were comparatively rare. Built by outside concerns and different individuals, their exact number and variations were never accurately recorded. But the few that survive are genuine museum pieces, representing a moment in history when the automobile took a giant leap forward, the sports car only a small step.

PIERCE ARROW

PRODUCTION SPAN
1904–1938

ENGINE
6-cyl in-line, sidevalve
T-head
8–cyl in-line sidevalve
80-degree V12 sidevalve

CAPACITY
13500cc/829ci
6300cc/386ci
7568cc/462ci

MAXIMUM POWER
80bhp @ 1200rpm
125bhp @ 3000rpm
175bhp @ 3600rpm

CHASSIS/SUSPENSION
All models: Pressed steel
channel section chassis
frame, semi-elliptic leaf
springs all round

BODY STYLE
Various

TOP SPEED
Various, dependent on
engine and body style
combination

The various products from Pierce Arrow are widely accepted as some of the finest luxury cars built in the United States. Given, though, the blurring of definitions concerning just what is and what is not a sports car, the sporting pretensions of even these larger cars are ample qualification. Engine sizes ranged from a straight six to much larger V12 units – so large, in fact, that these are among the biggest cars ever built in the USA.

The first model was the Pierce Great Arrow of 1904. It was built to reflect contemporary theory and practice, which demanded larger-capacity engines that revved slowly but delivered huge amounts of torque. By 1909 the Pierce engines had grown still further, ranging from between 350 and 650ci; the latter managed only 66hp. Capacity continued to grow, reaching a peak of 829 cubic inches (13.5 liters) by 1912. By then the Pierce Arrow had grown, too, with a 147in (373cm) wheelbase and a body made from heavy cast alloy.

About 1500 of these monsters were built until production ended in 1918. Then they concentrated on the rather smaller and more conservative type of vehicle which Detroit-based mass-production was making fashionable.

In 1928, the same year as its merger with the none-too-healthy Studebaker concern, Pierce Arrow made a return to the ranks of the high-performance builders with a new model aimed at reviving sales after the mid-twenties slump. Although it was only a modestly-sized 386ci straight eight, the timing for such a venture – a risk at the best of times – could hardly have been worse.

At first, sales were promisingly strong; 8,000 were shipped in 1929, the same number again in 1930, and a new and improved flagship model was on the stocks for 1931. This car should have carried the firm through the Depression years.

It was a good-looking device, with a 175hp, 462ci V12 of classic design, separate cast cylinder blocks and heads, and an alloy crankcase. But one new model wasn't enough to save Pierce Arrow at a time when so many other (and larger) names in the auto business were going to the wall.

Even companies that were small compared to the Big-Three had budget nameplates to fall back on, and with which to generate high volume and cash turnover. Cadillac, Packard — even Cord — all followed the same route for survival.

By 1933 the merger with Studebaker was over; Pierce Arrow was sold off before crippling losses could hurt the out-of-town independent. The Pierce-Arrow factory produced the Silver Arrow in that year, with an all-steel roof, running boards and 12-inch thick doors. It was quite a crowd-pleaser at the New York Car Show, but only five were ever built. The company was bought by a consortium which used every marketing trick in the book to bring it back into profit, but with little apparent success.

Despite Special Editions, record-breaking drives from "Mormon Meteor" Ab Jenkins and an offering of both large V12 limousines and smaller town cars, the sales graph continued on down from 1933. In 1934 2,000 cars were barely sold, and sales still declined, right through 1938, the year in which they stopped forever.

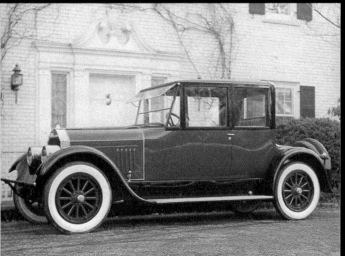

LEFT *The 1923 Pierce Arrow, a small and conservative model compared to the prewar monsters like the Great Arrow.*

CADILLAC V16

PRODUCTION SPAN
1930–37

ENGINE
45-degree V16

CAPACITY
7406cc/452ci

MAXIMUM POWER
165bhp @ 3400rpm

CHASSIS/SUSPENSION
Pressed steel chassis frame, semi-elliptic leaf springs all round

BODY STYLE
Coachbuilt, various

TOP SPEED
Max 90mph, dependent on body style

Cadillac is almost certainly the most widely respected American nameplate. Its only real rival is Lincoln, and both companies were founded by the same man: Henry Leland. His dream of quality caused a rift with his partner, who dreamed of cheap, mass-produced cars. As it turned out, both Leland and Ford were proved right.

The first Cadillac had a single-cylinder Ford engine, but later the V8 was adopted as the standard powerplant. The company pioneered electric lighting, and then the self-starter, and generally established the pattern that modern automobiles still follow. In 1909 Cadillac won the Dewar Trophy, an award made after three cars had been reduced to components and successfully reassembled from the mixture of parts. The Company adopted the slogan "Standard of the World" soon afterwards.

When Cadillac was absorbed into the still-growing GM in the same year as the Dewar Trophy was awarded, Leland departed, but Cadillac continued to grow in size and prestige. By the time of the Wall Street Crash they were already on the way to overtaking Packard as the top prestige nameplate. When that market collapsed in 1929, halving the number of car makers, Cadillac drew on the resources of the now-massive GM combine and survived into the mid-1930s in reasonably good shape.

The firm's flagship for this troubled decade had appeared late in 1929; while Cadillac created a small-car line (La Salle) in

BELOW LEFT *Henry Leland's emblem for Cadillac, 'Standard of the World'.*

ABOVE *The 1931 V16 Dual-Cowl Phaeton.*

LEFT *That excellent V16 engine was a masterpiece of design.*

order to insure survival, it continued the manufacture of prestige formal limousines. There were still a few people with money and for them Cadillac offered the superb V16. Built over an impressive 148in (376cm) wheelbase, Cadillac's exclusive coachbuilders, Fleetwood, created a wide range of truly breathtaking automobiles. By the end of the V16's run they had made 54 different body styles at prices ranging from $5,700 to $9,000.

At the heart of these cars was an immaculate new engine designed by Cadillac engineer Owen Nacker. It was an iron-block, 45-degree V16 that produced 165hp at 3400rpm out of 7.4 liters. With updraft carburetors, overhead valves and hydraulic tappets, it was a smooth and near-silent runner, a positive paragon of mechanical refinement and a serious rival to anything so far produced by Rolls-Royce.

At its launch, the V16 was presented as a rather formal Sedan de Ville, but the reserves of power and torque that the V16 delivered made it ideal for many applications, including much larger limousines and some fairly raffish gentlman's roadsters. Over the years, Fleetwood bodied the V16 as a Town Car, Sedanca, Dual Cowl Phaeton, a brilliantly sporting Cabriolet and the well-known "Madam X" sedans.

During the early Depression years, Cadillac sold the big V16 in good numbers, but sales gradually tailed off as the awful realities of war drew ever closer. In 1938 the excellent V16 was replaced by a lesser item, inferior in almost every respect, and that more or less signaled the end of the matter.

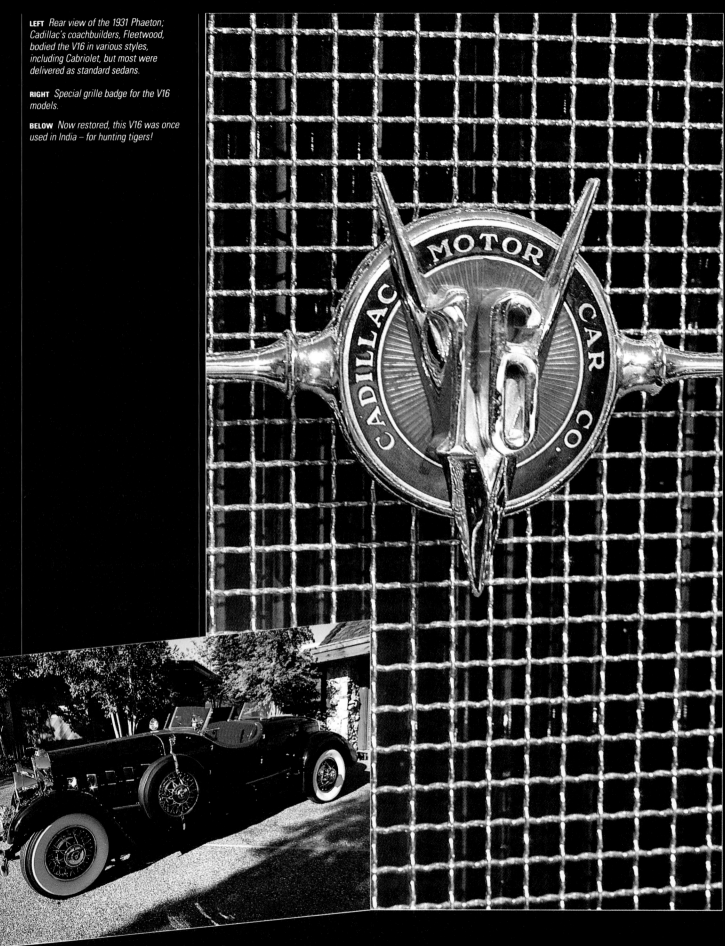

LEFT *Rear view of the 1931 Phaeton; Cadillac's coachbuilders, Fleetwood, bodied the V16 in various styles, including Cabriolet, but most were delivered as standard sedans.*

RIGHT *Special grille badge for the V16 models.*

BELOW *Now restored, this V16 was once used in India – for hunting tigers!*

AUBURN SPEEDSTER

PRODUCTION SPAN
1925–36

ENGINE
Supercharged 8–cyl in-line, aluminum head, ohv

CAPACITY
4587cc/280ci

MAXIMUM POWER
150bhp @ 4000rpm

CHASSIS/SUSPENSION
Pressed steel channel section chassis frame, half-elliptic leaf springs all round

BODY STYLE
2-seat convertible

TOP SPEED
100mph-plus

The Auburn Company, founded by the Eckert Brothers in Auburn, Indiana, in 1876, began as makers of fine carriages. It turned to the manufacture of uninspiring cars at the turn of the century, and managed to stay in business through the war years and into the 1920s. But in 1923 there was so much unsold inventory that they built only 175 cars. Then the firm's bankers approached Erret Cord, a Chicago businessman who had been successful selling Stewart McDonald's Moon Motor Cars, and asked whether he would be interested in helping.

On his first visit to the Auburn factory, Cord is said to have laughed aloud. But he made a deal anyway, in which he had a free hand but no wages. If he was successful, then he would be allowed to buy the controlling part of the company's stock at a favourable price. If he was unsuccessful, he got nothing.

Cord dropped all the prices, making the unsold Auburns cheaper than an equivalent Buick, and sold 2,226 cars in his first year. At the same time he gave the range a face-lift by adding what we would now call extra-cost options to each model to take care of the following year's sales, and began a longer-term reconstruction of the range, beginning with a new Lycoming straight eight. Later, Cord added Lycoming and other small suppliers to his growing empire.

Soon Auburn fortunes were climbing fast. The company was out of debt by the end of 1924, into profit by 1925, into record profit for 1926 and dividends by 1927, the year more than 14,000 cars left the plant. By now Cord had employed Gordon Buehrig and Harry Miller to work on the new Auburns; the first new cars Cord had produced for the company had been lower, sleeker and smarter than before, but were not the best that were to come. For most observers and enthusiasts, that honor fell to the superbly elegant 120 boat-tail Speedster, which made its debut in 1929. It took full advantage of the new Lycoming engine and established itself as a sporting car of considerable prowess, capturing a number of world records.

They had been established at Bonneville by race driver Ab "Mormon Meteor" Jenkins, when he roared across the salt flats at over 100mph (160km/hr) for 12 hours non-stop. To achieve that, the Lycoming engine had been mated to a supercharger produced by a new member of the Cord empire, Duesenberg. Production models of the Speedster were available with or without the blower, but those built with also had a written guarantee and a dash plaque certifying that the car had been individually tested at 100mph.

The Speedster was another car that became established as a classic almost on the same day it was first shown in public. Better still, the Speedster cost less than its big rival, the Stutz. Cord's timing for a low-priced sports car couldn't have been better, and during the following bad years the Speedster was an asset rather than a liability. When the selling on Wall Street began that October day in 1929 no manufacturer emerged un-harmed and some didn't emerge at all. But Auburn survived the Crash and the Great Depression; no mean feat in a period that saw auto production fall by half. Cord's low-priced "de-pression cars" kept the combine afloat. 1930 was a record year, 1931 even bigger. In the end it was not the Depression that closed Auburn down, but Cord's grand plans, which went down with a bang in 1937, taking the cars with it but leaving the successful Lycoming engine factory.

RIGHT *Gordon Buehrig's unmistakable styling for the Auburn Speedster.*

LEFT *The 'boat-tail' design was popular all over the world in the twenties and thirties.*

ABOVE *Another 'flying' emblem of the type that was popular between the wars.*

DUESENBERG MODEL J AND SJ

PRODUCTION SPAN

1928–38

ENGINE

8–cyl in-line, dohc, 4 valves per cylinder, detachable cast iron hemi-head (Supercharged on SJ model)

CAPACITY

6882cc/420ci

MAXIMUM POWER

265bhp @ 4250rpm (320bhp @ 4750rpm for SJ)

CHASSIS/SUSPENSION

Pressed steel channel section chassis with cross-bracing; front suspension by half-elliptic leaf springs, rear suspension by half-elliptic leaf springs and radius arms

BODY STYLE

Supplied as rolling chassis

TOP SPEED

110mph (J)
152mph (SJ)

Duesenberg just has to be one of the all-time classic sports cars the world has ever seen; the name is synonymous with superb engineering, ravishing good looks and tremendous power and speed. These cars, swept along on the crest of a wave that rolled all the way from Malibu beach, where the denizens of Hollywood's star-spangled orange groves whiled away their weekends, were the absolute pinnacle of 1930s sportsters.

The company was founded by two brothers, Fred and August Duesenberg, who came to the United States from Germany as children. Their first contact with the infant automobile was on the racetrack, although by then they were probably already building their own bicycles. The move into motor racing and their first practical experience of the internal combustion engine came in 1898, and they built their first car in 1903.

It was the start of a long and illustrious motor-racing history which linked Fred and Augie with most of the famous names of the period – people like Eddie Rickenbacker, for example – and put Duesenberg cars in the winner's circle at an even longer list of illustrious racing venues. In addition to well-documented wins at Indianapolis during the 1920s, a Duesenberg became the first – and still the only – American racing car to win the French Grand Prix.

The Duesenberg Company had been formed in 1912 to build race cars, and that success soon brought them to the building of road cars. The first was the 1920 Model A tourer, a car that encompassed all the knowledge and experience gained in competition. It quickly won itself an excellent reputation for performance and reliability.

The Model A's advanced features included widespread use of aluminum, as well as Duesenberg's new four-wheel hydraulic brakes. With a Duesenberg straight eight as well, it was fast, too, but expensive. Despite the price tag, continued race success insured continued demand, and soon the Duesenberg name was at the very top of a short list of exclusive sporting-car manufacturers. But ultimately, that didn't necessarily guarantee financial security, and Duesenberg was swept into the empire Erret Cord was building around himself and the Auburn Company.

Cord's benevolent stewardship began with a blank check that Duesenberg was instructed to expend on the design and construction of the fastest road car in the United States. Fred was a widely-renowned engineer, but Augie's design expertise

Erret Cord gave the Duesenberg brothers virtually unlimited funds and told them to build the best. The result was the supercharged Model SJ. With those huge exhaust outlet pipes (left) it's not difficult to spot that the engine is supercharged.

RIGHT AND FAR RIGHT *One of 125 Model J Duesenbergs bodied by Murphy; sold as a rolling chassis, the Model J was more expensive than a complete Rolls Royce from the Springfield, Mass., factory.*

ABOVE AND RIGHT *Duesenberg made two identical and very special Model J Roadsters, one for Al Jolson and this one, for Clark Gable.*

RIGHT AND PREVIOUS PAGE *Model JN Convertible: a breathtakingly beautiful and heartstoppingly expensive machine.*

was less well known. Between them, the brothers realized Cord's ambitions and created a classic that stood out from even their stable of classics – the magnificent Duesenberg Model J. Its breathtaking looks were matched in full by its supercharged performance, and with typical panache Cord completed the ensemble with an $8500 sticker price that was also quite breathtaking for the time.

The engine was a derivative of the new straight eight which Lycoming had built for Auburn, with dual overhead cams and four valves per cylinder. It produced a monstrous 265hp, giv-ing the Model J an impractical top speed of 116mph (185km/h) in two-seat touring coachwork. Even the four-seat Town Cars were 100mph (160km/h) – plus formal sedans. The Model J was everything Cord had asked for, and more. He found little trouble in selling it as a rolling chassis, even though the most expensive Packard available came complete with coachwork for less than $6,000. The wheelbase was either a never-ending 142.5in (362cm) or – to really stretch a point – 153.5in (390cm).

The optimism behind the creation of the Model J was mis-placed, and it arrived just as the 1929 Crash threatened to reduce drastically the number of potential customers. Luckily, Cord's survival plan, his "depression car", brought the combine safely through the worst, and Duesenberg rewarded him with a car that was even better still – the outstanding SJ. For the second time the Duesenberg badge was fixed to a sports roadster of extreme good looks and yet again the engineering was of the best as Fred created a car capable of about 130mph (208km/h).

Erret Cord fulfilled his part of the bargain again: the SJ chassis and engine cost almost $15,000. (The S in SJ = Supercharged.) And when it was bodied by the most expensive coachbuilders – Murphy, Le Baron and Derham were a few – a further $15,000 could be added to the price. But it was worth it, because they produced some of the most elegant cars ever seen, easily the equal of anything else produced in the USA or Europe at the time.

Fred Duesenberg died in a road accident in 1932. After the ACD combine failed in 1937, Augie tried – and failed – to revive the Duesenberg in 1947, and the marque was gone for ever.

FORD MODEL B

PRODUCTION SPAN
1932

ENGINE
45-degree L-head V8

CAPACITY
2228cc/135ci

MAXIMUM POWER
65bhp

CHASSIS/SUSPENSION
Pressed steel chassis frame,
box-section side members,
front and rear transverse
leaf springs

BODY STYLE
20 different styles available

TOP SPEED
80mph

0–50mph
12 seconds

Henry Ford had begun his career with race cars like Arrow and 999, and the vast numbers of Model Ts being built after 1908 become a familiar sight on the racetrack, since the sports car as such did not then exist. The Model T, stripped down, was as good a racer as anything else. Eventually even Henry saw that the Model T needed replacing, but the Model A that followed was not the successor nor the salvation Ford needed. Alfred Sloan's General Motors was drawing steadily away in the sales league, establishing a supremacy that still exists today.

The answer was a completely new car, and Ford went completely away from the earlier model, trying to squeeze too much innovation into one car in an attempt to recreate the Model T legend all over again. The car designated as its spiritual successor was the prosaically named Model B, a car destined to pass into legend for entirely different reasons than those Henry had hoped.

Now the Model B is regarded as *the* classic American car, especially by the hot-rodders who know it as the "Little Deuce Coupe" immortalized by the Beach Boys. Yet when it was launched, all that over-engineering made it something of an anticlimax; as a sales story it was only marginally less embarrassing for Ford than the Edsel, and for the next 30 years the car played second fiddle to the new engine launched as part of the package.

To begin with, the Model B was late. It should have appeared in the fall of 1931, but it wasn't even publicly announced until the spring of '32. It should have been available in up to 20 different body styles, but only a few were offered. It should also have had a choice of engines, and in that lay both the strength and weakness of the Model B.

With a new and stronger frame, its base engine was a revamped and more powerful version of the four-cylinder Model A engine. Add rubber engine mountings and a new synchromesh gearbox, and the Model B was altogether more modern and refined. New styling was based on the Model A, but was sleeker and looked still better with the low profile of the new

1932 Model B V8 Phaeton, probably built at the Trafford Park factory near Manchester, England.

100in (269cm) chassis. All of the 20 body styles of the Model A should have been carried over, and in addition, the Model B introduced a new three-window coupe shape: this was the car the Beach Boys sang about.

But introduction was delayed, while the engineers worked on developing Ford's new flathead V8 engine for production. It was worth waiting for, too; it would be the standard Ford engine for the next 32 years. Although in 1940 Ford introduced a mid-range straight six, the V8 was *the* performance option, far outclassing anything that was around in 1932 and continuing to be competitive right up to the launch of the Chevrolet small-block V8 in 1955.

The Henry Ford Museum in Dearborn, Michigan, has an eloquent testimonial to the power of the V8 penned by Clyde Barrow; Bonnie's boyfriend claimed he never stole anything else. It remained in production until it was replaced in 1953, by which time it was good for 110hp at 3800rpm. Its pinnacle was the hemi-head conversion designed by Zora Arkus Duntov. He took advantage of the strength of the bottom end, and allowed the venerable flathead to rev easily to 5,000rpm, pulling more than 500hp with a supercharger.

But in 1932, the new V8-engined cars were announced in February and officially on sale the next day. Demand was staggering; an estimated five million people called at Ford dealerships the first day it went on sale, but the production problems meant that there were hardly any cars available. By March only 1,100 cars had been built, all of them powered by the new V8.

By the time production of car and engine had been straightened out, demand for the car had more or less collapsed. The best month was June, when 43,000 V8s and 30,000 four-cylinders were built. But the Depression was beginning to bite, and sales of all new cars were dropping steadily. The last of the 1932 cars rolled from the line in February 1933, almost exactly one year after production had begun. The total build had fallen well below the planned one-and-a-half million; only 193,191 of the V8 cars and 89,036 of the four-cylinders were built, in all body styles.

KAISER DARRIN

PRODUCTION SPAN

1952–55 (100 cars sold after close-down)

ENGINE

6-cyl in-line by Kaiser/Frazer corp
V8 by Cadillac Division of General Motors

CAPACITY

3703cc/225ci (6-cyl)
5424cc/331ci (V8)

MAXIMUM POWER

118/140bhp (6-cyl)
250bhp (V8)

CHASSIS/SUSPENSION

Pressed steel box frame, coil & wishbone front suspension, semi-elliptic leaf spring rear suspension

BODY STYLE

Two-seat convertible

TOP SPEED

100mph (6-cyl)
140mph (V8)

When the war ended in 1945 Henry J Kaiser was anxious to experiment with a new material he believed was the key to the future of the automobile. He believed he could build cheap cars that would cost less than $1,000 by using GRP (fiberglass). Several prototypes were completed at the Kaiser laboratories in California, but his first postwar car was a more conventional unibody car produced in partnership with Joseph Frazer. Despite some grandiose plans for front-drive with torsion bar suspension, the Kaiser-Frazer of 1947 was a low-price version of the conventional rear-drive Frazer.

Built at Willow Run, where Ford had built wartime bombers, the car was an instant success, and made the new company the ninth-placed (and best independent) in the industry. But its lead was lost when the first new designs since 1942 appeared from Detroit; the best Kaiser-Frazer could do was a small face-lift. By 1954 production had fallen below 20,000 units, and in 1955 the company was wound up, showing a loss of $100 million.

Yet Kaiser had a good opportunity to revolutionize the car market, and he found the right material to do it. Both Ford and GM were planning to fight sports car imports from Europe with new products, and GM especially was interested in fiberglass as a basis for that attack.

GM design chief Harley Earl gave the GM project high priority after seeing, in 1952, a fiberglass two-seater designed by Howard 'Dutch' Darrin. It was the first practical, marketable automobile built in this new material. Darrin had been a designer of custom coachwork before the war, and decided to build his own cars when the war ended. He chose fiberglass as the material for a two-seat convertible and hoped to build 30,000 cars a year. His search for finance led him to the bankers who were underwriting the Kaiser-Frazer, and thus to Henry Kaiser himself.

Darrin's first prototype appeared in 1946 and used a 100hp Kaiser straight six engine, rectangular box frame and fiberglass bodywork. It was unique in a number of ways, not least for its complex hydraulic system which powered the seat adjustment, convertible top and four-wheel jacking system. Even the clamshell hood was raised hydraulically to expose the engine and front suspension.

Darrin's next project was a fiberglass-bodied two-seat sports car. Its two doors slid back to open, and the convertible landau top had a half-open position rather like a modern Targa top. Power again came from Kaiser-Frazer, with a choice of 226ci six rated at 140 or 118hp. There was also a smaller 161ci, 90hp Willys F-head unit that Darrin used for an incredible run of 60-plus prototypes. With a three-speed floorshift, top speed was fractionally less than 100mph (160km/h). When Henry Kaiser saw the first prototype, he was not immediately impressed, and, according to Darrin himself, stated quite flatly that his company was not in the business of building sports cars. The project was saved at that moment when Mrs Kaiser stepped forward: "Henry," she said, "This is the most beautiful thing I have ever seen."

At $3,668, it wasn't cheap compared to the imports like MG, Jaguar and Porsche, against which it would have to compete. Even Chevrolet's over-budget Corvette beat the Kaiser-Darrin on price. The glassfiber Corvette was in production in June of

RIGHT *Howard Darrin's striking but unsuccessful fiberglass sportscar. The Kaiser-Darrin's sliding doors were unique, but narrow openings made for difficult entry and exit.*

BELOW RIGHT *Note how the parking lights of the Kaiser-Darrin's seductive front end echo the shape of the grille.*

1953, the Kaiser-Darrin by early 1954. Neither car sold well. But Corvette had Chevrolet and GM behind it; the Kaiser-Darrin had neither. Just 435 were built during 1954, and none appeared during 1955, the year the company closed down.

The Kaiser-Darrin suffered the same problem as the GM sportster: it was hopelessly underpowered. GM had a new V8 coming, but Darrin had only his own resources to fall back on. He bought all the 100 or so uncompleted cars left when the factory was closed and gave them bigger, and more powerful Cadillac V8 engines. Thus equipped, the Kaiser-Darrins had a near-140mph (224km/h) top speed, but a matching sticker price – $4,350. Darrin sold them easily. Today, well over 300 Darrins are known to survive.

If he'd had the resources to build more he could perhaps have sold them. But even GM came close to axing Corvette, and, with small reserves, all independent makers were walking a financial tightrope. The outcome for Darrin was more or less inevitable.

CUNNINGHAM C4R

PRODUCTION SPAN
1951–55 (series)
1952 (C4R)

ENGINE
90-degree V8 by Chrysler
Corp

CAPACITY
5425cc/331ci

MAXIMUM POWER
300bhp @ 5200rpm

CHASSIS/SUSPENSION
Tubular spaceframe chassis,
independent front
suspension (coil &
wishbone), live rear axle
with coil springs and radius
arms

BODY STYLE
Two-seat open sports racing
car

TOP SPEED
Variable, according to tune

If Harry Stutz had a spiritual successor, then it was probably Briggs Cunningham. He was one of a handful of dedicated race enthusiasts who set out to produce a made-in-the-USA sports racing car that could meet the Europeans on equal terms. Cars like the Devin SS, the Bocar, the Reventlow and Scarab were among their products, but the buccaneering Cunningham had an advantage over all of them: Briggs Cunningham was a millionaire.

At the time a million dollars was a great deal of money: enough for Cunningham to become renowned as a yachtsman and car collector, and to fund a private Le Mans entry that could meet the best of the massively supported factory teams and be reasonably competitive. Cunningham's exploits are less well known outside the USA than in it; most of his share of the glory went to Shelby's Ford-backed Cobra, which had the money and the glamor of factory backing.

Cunningham, though, perfected the technique that had eluded the other would-be racers of the time, and established the ground rules for a racing and road-going ethos which would last for 30 years. What everyone was attempting to do – and Cunningham managed with considerable aplomb – was to mate the bottomless power resources of American-built V8 engines to an agile chassis equal to those being built in Europe. The Cunningham cars, to be fair, did not complete that marriage successfully; the chassis was always a problem (Cunningham built his own), and in the end it was the lack of development resources in this area alone which rendered his cars uncompetitive.

Like many of his contemporaries, Briggs Cunningham had a "relationship" with Detroit, which was so unofficial it could hardly be described as an arrangement. As a privateer, therefore, Cunningham's appearances at Le Mans are all the more creditable, and his was one of very few all-American efforts ever to be represented at the prestigious Sarthe circuit. Though the GT40 put Ford in the winner's circle it was heavily supported with British expertise, and the Cobras also owed much to the United Kingdom.

Cunningham began his assault on the prestige motor-race events of the world with a pair of Cadillacs. One was raced in more or less stock bodywork, but the other was given an admittedly basic sheet-metal two-seat body. Created for the occasion, it was to be the basis of the team's future products. This first attempt at sports car racing was not a raging success, but Cunningham was back the following year with a more committed team and cars that were created for racing rather than converted for it. The C2R, as the new car was called, featured a specially-built but rather heavy tubular chassis with a De Dion rear axle. The engines came from Chrysler, and the bodywork was similar to that of the earlier two-seater, although it followed the European style rather more closely.

The new cars went better than the previous year, and considering their background they stood up to the far more experienced European factory teams especially well. The philosophy of introducing the big-inch V8 powerplants into this class of racing gained immediate credibility from Cunningham's efforts, although it was clear that their forte was endurance rather than sprint events. This success encouraged Cunningham, and the following year the team produced what

RIGHT *The Cunningham C3 Continental Coupé was the road-going version of the racing cars Briggs Swift Cunningham had built to challenge the Europeans at Le Mans.*

BELOW RIGHT *Just 18 coupés and nine convertibles of the C3 were sold before production ceased in 1955; at Le Mans, the racing Cunninghams had gained fourth place in 1952 and third in 1953.*

most observers agree was its best-ever effort – the C4R.

Once again there was a tubular chassis with strong side members and small, lightweight cross-members. Compared to the racing chassis that were coming from Jaguar, Mercedes and Porsche, never mind Italy, it could hardly be considered state-of-the-art. Other considerations aside, the C4R weighed over a ton. But the engine – once more the all-conquering Chrysler smallblock hemi – overcame most of the weight disadvantage with its 300hp and 312lb/ft of torque, the latter peaking at a useful 2000rpm. Matched to a five-speed all-synchro gearbox, it made the C4R a very competitive sports car. It came close to

defeating the European products and almost gave Cunningham victory in only his third season of serious racing. The achievement this represented, when a comparative newcomer, a privateer as well, was outclassed only by Ferrari and Jaguar, was immeasurable. The C4R finished the 1952 Le Mans 24 hours in a remarkable fourth place, at an average of 88mph (141km/h).

The team finished third in 1953 with the C5, and third again (with the C4R) in 1954. But that was the end of the dream for Cunningham. The advances in chassis design effected by the big teams left the heavy and unwieldy Cunninghams at a serious disadvantage. Without the corporate backing – in talent and engineering resources as well as cash – Cunningham could not keep up the pace. The C6 of 1955 was more or less outclassed and marked the end of the line.

The same problem continued to handicap American racing efforts for many years to come, and that included the big names like Ford and GM as well as the privateers. But Cunningham had established a pattern, and he had proved how competitive the big V8 engines could be. Later on the technique was perfected by Shelby, who could only manage to remain competitive by using a European chassis. But in the mid-1950s the lack of chassis technology meant the end of the Cunningham team.

In addition to laying a racing foundation, Cunningham also provided a spur to the big factories with the road-going versions of his race cars. Very few of the Michelotti-styled C3 cars were built, but their very existence proved that Americans could successfully build a road-going sports car which could compete realistically with the smaller European cars so increasingly popular after World War II.

CHEVROLET CORVETTE

PRODUCTION SPAN

1953 to date

ENGINE

6-cyl ohv in-line
90-degree V8

CAPACITY

L6 3850cc/235ci
V8 4342cc/265ci
V8 4637cc/283ci
V8 5358cc/327ci
V8 5735cc/350ci
V8 6489cc/396ci
V8 6997cc/427ci

MAXIMUM POWER

L6 235ci/150bhp
V8 265ci/162/225bhp
V8 283ci/220/245/270/250/
283/290/315bhp
V8 327ci/250/300/340/360/
395/350bhp
V8 350ci/265/320/330/
335bhp
V8 396ci/425bhp
V8 427ci/390/425/435/
460bhp

CHASSIS/SUSPENSION

Steel frame, front
suspension coil spring and
wishbone, rear suspension
by semi-elliptic leaf spring,
changing to independent
with transverse leaf in 1964;
rear leaf fiberglass from
1981; new backbone chassis
from 1984 with fiberglass
leaf spring suspension

BODY STYLE

Two-seat sports coupe and
convertible

TOP SPEED

1955: 108mph
1968: 150mph
1988: 150mph

0–60mph

1955: 11.1 seconds
1967: 5.5 seconds
1988: 6.8 seconds

The definition of a sports car is never easy. There are few cars which all observers would agree fit the bill, and in general they tend to be of European, if not Italian, extraction. The list of American-built sports cars that fit into this sort of category is perhaps the shortest of all, with only two names that are guaranteed instant worldwide recognition. One is Shelby, of course, but it is Corvette that springs to mind first. Launched as a low-price competitor to the European imports in 1953, Corvette's status and legend have grown over the past 30 years. Today it's no longer the USA's only volume-built sports car (although it was the first), but instead is America's first – and only – supercar.

From Day One Corvette was genuinely innovative, almost experimental at times. It has established industry firsts, precedents and standards, and is now deep in the race to put the world's first active ride-suspension system into production. For a car that didn't make it past its first year and went several years before meeting volume targets or making a profit, it's an impressive set of achievements.

Russian engineer Zora Arkus Duntov is the man most often described as the "father" of the Corvette, but it's a misleading title. When Duntov gave up his racing career and joined GM as a research engineer in May 1953, Corvette had already been seen at the January Motorama, and Job One came off the ersatz production line set up in a corner of the Flint, Michigan factory just four weeks later.

But Duntov's interest in racing drew him and Corvette ever closer, and as the years went by his interest in the car became more and more paternal. His first work on Corvette was to sort out the handling, cleaning up tail-end behavior and giving it firmer grip. However, there was little he could do about the performance; early Corvette engines were nothing more exciting than a dressed-up version of an old and fairly uninspiring straight six truck engine which had its roots back in 1929. Along

RIGHT *1954/5 Corvette in Sportsman red.*

BELOW *One of the 300 Polo White Corvettes to be built at Flint, Michigan, in 1953.*

with mediocre two-speed automatic transmission and suspension taken right off the Chevy sedans, Corvette was initially a marketing man's sports car rather than a driver's. The whole point was that it *looked* the part.

However, that was where it ended, and the sports car enthusiasts gave it a determined thumbs-down. They weren't unfair; underpowered and loose-handling, it was far from perfect. But with Duntov's suspension work it got better, and with the 1955 debut of Ed Cole's brilliant smallblock, Chevrolet's first V8 for more than 30 years, Corvette's popularity suddenly took off.

The bulk of the credit must go to the superb 265 V8; in later years it became a 283, 302, 327 and finally the standard 350ci powerplant of the GM range. More than 40 million of these engines have been built, making it the most successful power unit in history. It remains the standard Corvette powerplant until the 1990s, and will remain the favorite performance option for much, much longer than that.

Despite all of that, GM was not geared to high-quality, low-volume manufacture, and Corvette sales could have been

better. Even with a V8, accountancy still would have killed it off in 1955 – except that Ford produced its Thunderbird and GM would not leave the market to give Ford a clean sweep.

So GM persisted with Corvette, even though it was far from being a financial winner. Duntov and the Chevrolet engineers worked hard at making it a race winner, and the 283 overbore and Rochester fuel-injection kit which appeared on the 1957 cars were prompted by competition needs rather than market demand. Still, it gave Corvette another new lease on life; with one horsepower for every cubic inch of capacity, the fuel-injection cars were formidable performers.

Then in 1963 it got another boost from the new design produced under the direction of Bill Mitchell. There was much talk of a mid-engine Corvette, and designs had progressed quite a long way, but eventually the cost of engineering the transaxle meant the project was scrapped. Instead the 1963 cars gained

the looks of a one-off race car, which Mitchell had campaigned privately and called Sting Ray.

The Corvette of the same name, with pop-up headlights, split rear screen and sharp, pointed styling, was an instant winner. Its new Independent Rear Suspension, the disc brakes it acquired the following year and the later arrival of the new big-block V8 made it a true performer as well. When the Grand Sports cars wiped the floor with the Cobras at Nassau, Corvette's place in legend was assured. And since you could, by clever use of an order blank and the option boxes, order a 150mph (240km/h)-plus Corvette right off the showroom floor, its place on the street was also assured.

With that kind of performance, it was no surprise that Sting Ray needed disc brakes, not that its introduction was delayed until something powerful enough could be developed. When they were ready for use, the new four-wheel discs outran the

LEFT *Famous for its heavy use of unnecessary chrome and criticized because of it, the 1958 Corvette remains a collectors' favorite.*

BELOW LEFT *1963, the new look, and that controversial split-window coupe.*

ABOVE *The 1965 Corvette convertible.*

BELOW *The 1968 re-style, longest-serving of all the Corvette body shapes, and the best known.*

ABOVE LEFT *In 1981 the Corvette front end gained a new, integrated spoiler.*

ABOVE *A deep chin spoiler had been added to earlier late seventies models as an after-market accessory.*

BELOW *The long-awaited 'new' Corvette arrived in 1984 (no Corvettes were built in 1983). The clamshell hood reveals the familiar 350V8.*

standard Chevrolet brake abuse course, and a new, tougher, circuit had to be designed to take them to the limit. Even today, standard Corvette disc brakes are among the very best available on any sports car anywhere in the world.

In 1968 Corvette again got new looks. This time, along with the sweeping lines penned by Larry Shinoda, it got a new chassis too, and entered the longest and most stable phase of its career. From 1968 to 1983, the new Corvette, with its plastic nosecone and rear end, stayed in production virtually unchanged. All the time it could sell every car that was being built, Chevrolet, deep in John DeLorean's cost-cutting return to profitability exercise, was unlikely to change anything but the sticker price. That climbed steadily over the years, and Corvette at last began to repay, in pure financial terms, all the time, effort and investment it had swallowed.

Despite the fact that the cars making it to the street in that time remained the same, Corvette development work behind the scenes continued at a fast pace. Duntov had been convinced that mid-engine was the layout to have many years before and continued to press for its adoption. Though there were many attractive show and experimental cars – and almost as many rumors – the mid-engined Aerovette missed out, thanks to the tooling costs of the transaxle once again. At one time GM's flirtation with the rotary engine – inspired and led by Ed Cole – looked as though it could swing the balance, and two show cars were built, but the Wankel couldn't meet long-term emission regulations, and Corvette stayed the same yet again.

Finally the long-awaited (and as widely rumored) Corvette restyle arrived in 1984. GM sacrificed the chance of a 30-year anniversary model by having no 1983 Corvette at all. Instead production moved to a new facility at Bowling Green, Kentucky, and the new cars were built there. Styled by Jerry Palmer, under the leadership of Chief Engineer Dave McLellan (who replaced Duntov), the new Corvette had a low, flat, wind-cheating body, a reworked 350 V8 engine and a healthy $25,000 sticker price. When the 1985 cars were released with a 150mph (240km/h) top speed, Corvette became a fully paid-up member of the supercar league, a position likely to be increased by a 170mph (272km/h) Corvette – which could be with us soon.

ABOVE *The new clamshell hood gives superb access to the 350 V8 and shows off the new aluminum suspension components.*

LEFT *Seen with each of the.major body changes throughout its then 31-year lifespan, the new Corvette appeared in 1984, and retained the flavor of its prestigious forbears, with distinct styling cues such as pop-up headlamps and round tail lamps (opposite).*

FORD
THUNDERBIRD

PRODUCTION SPAN
1955 to date

ENGINE
'Y-block' V8 variants

CAPACITY
4785cc/292ci
5112cc/312ci
5768cc/352ci
7046cc/430ci
6390cc/390ci
7013cc/428ci
7030cc/429ci

MAXIMUM POWER
292ci: 193/198bhp
312ci: 202/215/225/245/270/
285/300bhp
352ci: 300bhp
430ci: 350bhp
390ci: 300/315/340bhp
428ci: 345bhp
429ci: 360bhp

CHASSIS/SUSPENSION
Pressed steel chassis frame,
independent front
suspension by wishbones &
coil springs, rear suspension
by half-elliptic leaf springs
(1955–7)
Unibody construction from
1958 onwards

BODY STYLE
Two-seat sports 1955–7
Four-seat 'Personal Car'
1958–69
Family sedan 1970 to date

TOP SPEED
Various

Though Ford's flathead V8 had been *the* performance engine since 1932, the company had never made anything, outside of its short run of V8 roadsters in 1932, which could be called a sports car.

But in the early 1950s, stung by the European imports, the low-volume sports racers being built in the USA and, finally, by the launch of the Corvette in 1953, Ford had to react. The answer was an all-time classic almost immediately. Ford had gotten its numbers right, and the Thunderbird was everything the market had been waiting for.

That's hardly a surprise; Ford had taken note of the sporting element that stole the show at the 1951 Paris Salon, and, in fact, T-Bird had been on the drawing board since that time. But while the sketches were being made the Ford marketing men, with typical thoroughness, were delving into the marketplace and coming up with a clear picture of the kind of sports car Americans wanted to drive.

Their technique was evident right from the word go; while Corvette was the embodiment of a few enthusiasts who won corporate approval of their dreams, Thunderbird was a con-

RIGHT *1957 Thunderbird Convertible, last of the classic 55-57 models.*

BELOW *With optional hardtop and 'portable' side window, plus continental kit for spare tire stowage, the Thunderbird was strikingly handsome.*

sidered and hard-hitting attempt to sell cars. It worked.

The specification of the '55 T-Bird left its GM rival for dead. Early Corvettes had an old GM truck engine with as much new life as it could stand breathed into it, matched to a dull two-speed automatic box. T-Bird arrived in the showroom with Ford's new 289 Y-block V8 and a choice of manual gearbox with overdrive or automatic transmission; it was styled in Frank Hershey's studio and, also in keeping with the market research findings, it was bigger than Corvette and priced just a little bit higher.

For the next three years the Thunderbird lasted in more or less the same shape, although as the seasons passed small additions and changes were made in proper Detroit fashion. The result of those changes was to make one model seem more elegant than all the others, and to create what amounted to an "instant classic" – the 1957 Thunderbird hardtop with continental kit.

The '56 models had sprouted the kit, which put the spare tire out between the deck lid and the rear bumper in response to complaints about lack of trunk space. It was the location chosen by Edsel Ford for his personal Lincoln, which was later named after the technique that Edsel said made the Lincoln look more "continental".

Even the porthole styling in the detachable hardtop, created by Ford stylist Bill Poyer, had first been seen on the '56 cars, and this too was a carry-over for 1957. In addition, the small '56 tailfins gained extra emphasis, in keeping with the fashion established by Harley Earl on Cadillac – and which still hadn't reached their awesome peak.

For 1957 Thunderbird got more power too; the 292 V8 was upped in capacity and power to 312ci, and was even offered with a blower, which pushed it up to 300hp. As T-Bird and Corvette battled it out at the Daytona Speed Weeks, they came away with honors more or less even, but the GM engineers had

by then put in a lot of work on fuel injection, and there was a definite tendency to "bend" rules about standard specification as far as possible.

Then in 1958 more market research made Ford change tack; Thunderbird was transformed, growing from a two-seat sports cars to a big four-place convertible that Ford dubbed it "Personal Car". With a new unibody riding a 113in (287cm) wheelbase, T-Bird was something of a monster. But market research proved right again; despite their apparently unwieldy size, the big '58 cars sold almost double what the '57 had managed. In '59 they did better still, and the styling carried through almost unchanged for a third year.

A new 352ci V8 gave standard models 300hp, and there was a 350hp, 430ci big-block option as well. But when the styling cycle changed in 1961 and the long, droop-snoot look appeared, sales started to fall away, and continued to slide. Despite the research, Ford dealers were besieged by requests for another two-seat Thunderbird, and this constant barrage of demand was something that front line sales executive Lee Iacocca would remember when he became Chief Executive. His memory would later prompt the true successor to the '57 Thunderbird in 1965, and Ford would call it Mustang.

Meantime, Iacocca authorized a two-seat styling exercise based on the 1962 car; it appeared as the 1963 Sports Roadster, with a fiberglass tonneau cover designed by stylist Bud Kaufmann. It clipped behind the front seats, contained "streamliner" headrests for the front passengers and allowed the soft top to be raised and lowered while it was in place. The conversion added $650 to the price of a car that cost less than $5,000, making it a rarely chosen option, though it was available for the next season as well. The 1964 face-lift made T-Bird heavier still, and with the 1965 debut of the Mustang the Thunderbird swung up-market as a luxury sedan. Today the name carries no more than a hint of former glories.

PONTIAC GTO

PRODUCTION SPAN

1964–71

ENGINE

90-degree ohv V8

CAPACITY

6374cc/389ci

MAXIMUM POWER

325/348bhp

CHASSIS/SUSPENSION

Unitary chassis, torsion bar propshaft and transaxle, independent link-type rear suspension

BODY STYLE

Four/five seat saloon and convertible

TOP SPEED

Variable

0–100mph

'Standard' 389 11.8 seconds (*Car and Driver*, 1964)

While there's plenty of controversy about exactly how to define a sports car, there's no such problem dealing with North American's special contribution to the world of high-performance motoring: the musclecar.

Fittingly, it was a marketing exercise rather than some purist dream of excellence which created the breed; it came from Detroit and was the first tangible evidence of the strength that the young consumer would develop in Western society. The musclecar was, if you like, a product of the postwar baby boom.

The emergence of that young market was spotted by Pontiac's general manager Simon "Bunkie" Knudsen. When he took over Pontiac it was on a downhill run, the old-maid division of GM with a falling sales graph and possible closure just around the corner. Knudsen's job was to turn Pontiac around, and he did it through performance and through his recognition that the growing youth market represented a massive area of potential growth. Knudsen pointed Pontiac straight at it, even though much of his target audience was till too young to hold a driver's license. His attack was based on a "Super Duty" version of the new smallblock V8 and from 1955 on, Pontiac's 300hp, 130mph stormers took NASCAR, NHRA and Daytona by storm.

When the 1957 AMA no-race edict came into force, Pontiac was in trouble. Unable to race or to advertise performance, the company couldn't promote any of its catalog of performance parts. Available from the factory, these performance packages, fitted through the dealership program, had pushed Pontiac from number six to number three in the new car sales league.

Knudsen ignored the performance ban as long as he could. But in 1963 some of the Corvette group's racing activities became too well publicized, and GM issued its own no-race edict in very clear terms. Pontiac needed a new angle, and it was dreamed up by advertising man Jim Wangers and John DeLorean. They proposed putting the big 389 V8 into the Tempest, a four-cylinder compact that was the smallest vehicle in the range. It was little more than a hot-rod technique, an area Detroit had never been too proud to learn from. However the GM no-race memo underlined some very strict corporate policy on power-to-weight ratios which strictly limited the size of engine that could be fitted into any of the division's products.

The proposed new car was wildly out of line with that policy, and was developed in near-secrecy by a chosen few. Pontiac chief engineer Pete Estes was deeply involved, but he kept the car secret too; the rules said that the Tempest could not have an engine larger than 330ci. Even when it did break cover, the "conspirators" showed it to the Board as a 326, with the bigger 389 offered only as an option. Even then the reaction was violent; participants say it came close to degenerating into a fistfight. The Board assured DeLorean that the car would never sell, but they couldn't stop the program going ahead. The secret had somehow been leaked, and dealers were beginning to send in orders. A compromise decision allowed a limited build of 5,000 units, but in its first year it sold 32,000, and became Pontiac's most successful model introduction. Wangers and DeLorean believed they could have sold twice that number, and the following year they did exactly that.

The car was called the Tempest GTO; at this stage it was not a car in its own right, just a series of high-performance options.

RIGHT *Horribly mutilated version of a 1970 GTO Judge, itself a last-ditch attempt to keep the GTO myth alive.*

BELOW RIGHT *The GTO was an option on the Pontiac Tempest, ordinarily just a family compact.*

This became the established format for the musclecar, the performance phenomenon Pontiac had just invented. Even the 389 engine that was the basis of the GTO was option 320, and some buyers didn't even notice it on the order blank.

The first GTO – and its lack of ground-up design – came in for a lot of criticism. From any angle, it was just a five-seat sedan with a huge engine, giving it staggering performance, although only in one direction – forward. Turning and stopping were rated less important than its dummy hood scoops and triangular, red, white and blue GTO badges. To be fair there was a mandatory suspension kit which went some way to coping with the power the engine could deliver, but disc brakes were not forced on buyers – in fact they weren't available.

But GTO owners could choose from a list of options that let them tailor a car with almost any number of personal specifications. There were cosmetics like a center console, and real performance add-ons such as the Hurst floor shift or the amaz-

ing three-carburetor Tri-Power manifold pack. This ran only the center carburetor up to around 100mph, then (and under hard acceleration) the two other carbs started pumping gas into the top of the manifold, giving the GTO a noticeable power surge around 3,300rpm.

The GTO quickly built up its own myth and became the subject of many pop songs; GM eventually got Ronnie and the Daytonas to produce an "in-house" version in answer to people like Jan and Dean jumping on the bandwagon. Then there was GTO cologne, cuff-links, tie bar, sports jacket, socks – even shoes specially designed for driving GTOs in. The GTO began to appear on TV programs like *My Three Sons*, but made its biggest hit as the Dean Jeffries special "Monkeemobile", which arrived at the height of Monkeemania. Each member of the Monkees pop group was given a GTO for personal use, and PR hype hit an all-time high when Mike Nesmith was stopped on the Hollywood Freeway after clocking 125mph (200km/h).

ABOVE *1967 GTO; an option on the order book which created a whole new marketing strategy. Not surprisingly, the GTO is a firm favorite in the customizing market, transforming into such exotica as this beast (left), with blown engine, flanked by a Chevy Impala.*

FORD MUSTANG

PRODUCTION SPAN
1964 to date

ENGINE
6-cyl ohv, 90-degree Y-block V8

CAPACITY
L6 2785cc/170ci
L6 3277cc/200ci
V8 4260cc/260ci
V8 4735cc/289ci
V8 6390cc/390ci
V8 4948cc/302ci
V8 6997cc/427ci
V8 5751cc/351ci
V8 7013cc/428ci
V8 7030cc/429ci

MAXIMUM POWER
170ci/101bhp
200ci/120bhp
260ci/164bhp
289ci/200/225/271bhp
390ci/320/335bhp
302ci/230/220bhp
427ci/390bhp
351ci/250/290/300bhp
428ci/335bhp
429ci/375bhp

CHASSIS/SUSPENSION
Unibody construction, independent front suspension by coil springs, semi-elliptic rear springs

BODY STYLE
Variable

TOP SPEED
Variable

When Ford followed the advice of its research gurus and upsized Thunderbird into the "Personal Car" market, Lee Iacocca had been a front-line salesman. Now, as Company President, he got Ford to look into the two-seat market once again, with a view to resurrecting the Thunderbird as a two-seat sports car. The move was completely in keeping with the massive change in marketing thrust that was about to take place. In April of 1963, Iacocca made his now-famous speech declaring Ford's commitment to "Total Performance" – a flagrant rejection of the AMA no-race edict of 1957.

The Total Performance program had as its central support the need to develop a race program that could "father" a performance-oriented production car. As far back as 1961 a prototype had been put together with initial parameters that were almost a straight lift from the Corvette ethos of ten years earlier. The new car was meant to be small, fast and nimble, and to have a sticker price of around $2,500. Projected volume for the first year was 100,000 units, and it was expected to continue selling at that rate.

The first prototype was a little too radical to fit the brief, especially on price. It used a mid-mounted V4 taken from Cardinal, although the layout had already been disqualified for Corvette replacement on grounds of cost. Coincidentally, it used a wedge-shaped fiberglass body. From any angle it involved too many new materials and too much tooling; and was rejected almost immediately simply because on cost alone it could never be a profitable production car. More prototypes were built, until finally Iacocca saw the T-Bird successor he was looking for. The shape he chose retained many of the styling cues of that first prototype, but was a conventional front-engine, rear-drive lay-out.

BELOW AND RIGHT *The Mustang was a sensation at its launch, providing Ford with its most successful first-year model sales ever.*

BELOW RIGHT *By 1970 the Mustang had put on extra weight and inches.*

The production prototype rode a fairly long 108in (274cm) chassis, was a four-seater (not the two-seater that dealers were screaming for – had been, in fact, since 1957) and ran a 170ci Falcon straight six or a 260 V8. Styling came from David Ash, Joe Oros and Gayle Halderman in Ford's design studio, and it established the classic lines for what would soon be named the "ponycar" in its honor. That first design would be slavishly copied for at least the next decade and still be the baseline 20 years on. In 1965, though, it came as something of a shock, and the rest of Detroit had to move faster than it was used to in order to catch up.

That was something they never did, though. Ford had stolen a two-year marketing lead and its new car stormed onto the streets at a phenomenal pace. In the end the Thunderbird designation was dropped, and it bore a brand new name. Making its debut in April of 1965, the Mustang was Ford's most successful first-year model ever.

In fact, the Mustang was the biggest success story of the 1960s, selling 680,000 units in its first nine months of production and setting an all-time record for first-year sales by *any* manufacturer. Part of that success stemmed from the choice of body styles; Mustang came as a hardtop, a convertible or a fastback coupe, and those options were virtually unchanged for years. Within six months of launch it had grown plenty of power choice as well, and included a 120hp 200ci six or the bored-out 289 V8, which delivered 200, 225 or 271hp. For Mustang this was just the start of the horsepower race.

Like the musclecars, Mustang's success story was concealed in the option boxes on the dealer order blanks. It came as a fairly basic compact, but clever placing of tick marks meant that

you could order a full-house race car by adding things like three- or four-speed stick shifts, handling package, disc brakes, power steering, air-conditioning, tachometer, bucket seats and, naturally enough, a selection of special badgework, stripes and body moldings.

The convertibles sold well to begin with (100,000 in 1965) but began to decline gradually in keeping with the general trend in the market more or less forced by Federal regulations on impact strength. By 1970 only 7,000 Mustang convertibles were sold. The fastback was popular – 77,000 in 1965 – but the real star was the notchback: 500,000 sold in the first year.

Those ratios were much the same in the second year, when once again Mustang had a whole new sales arena all to itself. Although total sales were slightly down, 607,568 units still represented a staggering achievement, well beyond even Iaccoca's expectations. The hardtop coupe led the pack with almost half a million sold, the convertible was a very poor second at 72,119, and Steven McQueen's Bullit-shape fastback came a poor third – 35,698. But this was the last year Mustang had the market to itself, and in 1967 it had to face competition from the rest of the industry, most notably the GM reply in the shape of Camaro and Firebird.

Total Mustang sales were down to 472,121 as Camaro and Firebird combined sold 303,475, with the larger percentage just going to the Chevrolet. Mustang even had to face an in-house rival that year, too, as Ford introduced its up-market Mercury Cougar, which was really just a bigger and plusher Mustang. To boost the falling sales, Ford gave Mustang its first taste of real power outside of that installed by Shelby. The big-block engines, a 335hp 390ci and a 390hp 427, came in 1968.

and turned the 1968 cars into good-looking, fast cars – which were just what the musclecar-oriented market was begging for.

Then 1969 brought a big face-lift, allowing a glimpse of what was to come as Mustang grew longer, lower and wider, sprouted dummy hood scoops and vents and a rear deck spoiler. Of more interest to performance-minded drivers was the new 351 smallblock V8, which provided 250 or 290hp. This was, however, the year that low-compression engines became a reality and the output of the big-block engines fell from 390 to 320hp, and from 428 to 335hp.

By 1970 the new Mustangs were marketing tricks rather than new sports cars. The Boss Mustangs entered the decade alongside the Mach 1 with a total of six body styles. The hardtop coupe was still the favorite, but total sales were right down below 200,000. The Camaro/Firebird total was also down, reflecting the gradual trend away from performance.

The Boss was intended to be the new Mustang flagship, replacing the previous top-line Shelby cars. Therefore it was the Boss which got Ford's semi-hemi Cobra-Jet NASCAR engine for street use. It lifted power by comparison to previous Mustangs, giving the big-block 375hp, almost as much as the pre-smog engines and quite fast enough for street use. It was only one of seven engine options, though, beginning with the 200ci straight six.

But the performance decade was over: in late 1970 Ford abandoned most of its Trans Am, USAC and NASCAR program, and Mustang soldiered on as something of a toothless wonder until the 1980s, when suddenly performance was no longer a dirty word in Detroit and the big names went back to the race tracks. Now Mustang and Corvette are meeting in anger again, although the race vehicles bear little relationship to today's road cars.

PONTIAC FIREBIRD

PRODUCTION SPAN
1967 to date

ENGINE
6-cyl ohv in-line
90-degree V8

CAPACITY
L6 3769cc/230ci
V8 5342cc/326ci
V8 5735cc/350ci
V8 6554cc/400ci

MAXIMUM POWER
L6 230ci/155/165/175/
215bhp
V8 326ci/250/285bhp
V8 350ci/265/320/330/
375bhp
V8 400ci/330/335/345 bhp

CHASSIS/SUSPENSION
Unibody construction;
independent front
suspension by coil springs
and wishbones; rear
suspension by semi-elliptic
leaf springs

BODY STYLE
Four-seat sports coupe

TOP SPEED
Variable according to
engine

When Mustang caught GM napping, the pressure to respond quickly was vast; the answer was the F-car, and responsibility for its design went to Chevrolet, which produced the Camaro. Over at Pontiac, there were a number of people who felt that they, as creators of the Tempest and the GTO, ought not to be seen following when performance cars were discussed. They had even gone so far as to produce a prototype two-seater based around Corvette and designated XP-833. Later, with changes to lighting and grille, it would hit the streets as the 1968 face-lift for Corvette. But in 1965 it was still a secret, even when two cars were built. And although Pontiac wanted this car as its own Mustang-basher, it eventually wound up with what should have been a Camaro clone – Firebird.

And Camaro itself was already so late that the Firebird was based almost entirely on the 1968 Nova, which is why it was tall around the A-pillar and short along the hood, completely at odds with the ponycar style established by Ford. Although Chevrolet was pleased with the car, Pontiac wasn't, so it gave Firebird bigger wheels and tires, and lowered the suspension, adding traction bars to improve handling further.

Slightly more expensive than Mustang and Camaro, Firebird also had an optional 400ci V8 that pushed it into the luxury bracket. But the big engine was not the 360-horse option on GTO, but a mild 335hp item, which was actually just a governed version of the GTO engine that could be de-restricted by anyone with a screwdriver and ten seconds to spare. In 1968 came the Firebird 400 HO (High Output), with three-speed automatic to replace the two-speed common to most GM applications at the time. Properly sorted, Firebird was now a fast, clean-handling car that was well-liked by magazine road-testers and the buying public – although it was an expensive choice in the muscle marketplace of the late sixties.

Despite that, Firebird sold well, 50,000 within ten weeks of its launch, and the first 12 months' sales topped 113,000, compared to Camaro's 200,000-plus, an accurate reflection of the predetermined 60/30 split GM had allocated between the two divisions. The next year saw the 400 HO engine become a Ram Air HO 11, developing 340 in Firebird.

In 1969 came the first major face-lift for what was still a reasonably new car. Firebird put on 2in in length and spread out at the rear to a 60in (152cm) track. It was also the year Firebird got its first one-piece plastic front, although the GM Endura soft noses featured on the Corvette were considered too expensive; Firebird and Camaro had Lexan, which was cheaper, and rock-hard.

There was a new version of the 400 Ram Air, with four-bolt mains, forged aluminum pistons, heavy-duty rockers, aluminum intake manifold and a wild cam. It was rated at only 345 bhp, but once again there was a great deal more power available to anyone with a screwdriver. In any case, this was the era when auto makers began to conceal the true performance capabilities of their engines.

This car was a serious piece of street-racing equipment, confined to the street rather than the racetrack it was planned for by the now-strictly enforced GM no-race edict. But it still wasn't the ultimate Firebird, which was just around the corner. And that would begin life as an option on the order blank and grow into a complete new marque – Trans Am.

RIGHT *The Z-28 name lived on after 1969 as a marketing tool, in which guise it was very successful. Only a few hundred rear race cars were sold, but thousands of badged-up Camaros with no real power, like this one, hit the streets.*

BELOW RIGHT *In 1968 the Camaro was available with another performance option, the RS package, part of a series of options that was the longest in Detroit.*

CHEVROLET CAMARO Z28

PRODUCTION SPAN
1968–1984
(following data for 1968 model)

ENGINE
90-degree V8

CAPACITY
4948cc/302ci

MAXIMUM POWER
290bhp @ 5800rpm

CHASSIS/SUSPENSION
Unibody construction with coil spring and wishbone independent front suspension, semi-elliptic leaf spring rear suspension

BODY STYLE
Four-seat sports coupe

TOP SPEED
140-mph plus

Arguably GM can claim that the Corvette was the first true postwar sports car built in the United States; certainly it was the first built in any volume. The newness of the concept to American drivers showed quite quickly. Despite the publicity that an influx of sporty European cars had generated, Corvette was a first-year flop.

Even so, Ford followed quickly with Thunderbird, demonstrating superior marketing skills by outselling Corvette two to one from Day One and immediately getting out of the sports car market by upsizing T-Bird when they saw it had little growth potential.

Ford's return to the market in the mid-1960s caught the rest of Detroit by surprise (by industry standards, at least), even though by 1965 the advent of the GTO and the musclecar had quite clearly shown that the youth market was definitely performance-oriented. But Mustang was launched with a head-start of two clear seasons before the other manufacturers caught up.

Bill Mitchell was head of GM Art and Design, and overall responsibility for the Chevrolet response fell within his brief. The design produced followed to the letter the classic ponycar mold established by Mustang, which meant a low roofline, long hood, short deck, flat nose and squared-off deck. Chevrolet called it Camaro, and it was in the works in time for the 1967 model year.

Camaro followed the classic musclecar marketing technique, which Mustang had developed almost into an art form. Its massively long option list included no less than 81 factory-fitted choices and an additional 41 dealer-installed accessories. The idea was that it allowed every buyer to tailor their new car to an exact and individual specification. Americans bought it in increasingly large numbers, and within months the Camaro was available in more different specifications than any other car in production at the time.

The Camaro base engine was a 140hp straight six, and naturally there was a more powerful 155hp version available as an option, as well as two V8 engines, the superb 327 and, exclusive to Camaro in its launch year, a new 350 smallblock which was destined to become the standard GM powerplant within a few years.

There was also another V8 option available to Camaro buyers. Buried at the bottom of the order blank was option Z-28. The well-informed few who checked this box were getting their hands on a race-ready engine designed for the Trans Am series by veteran Chevrolet competition engineer Vince Piggins. (Even though GM had officially backed out of motor sport in 1957, there were still plenty of engineers who were curious about racing as a development test bed and used it solely for that purpose.)

The new 302 engine just squeezed Camaro into Group 2 of the Trans Am series, which had a top limit of 305ci. And since the strict FIA rules demanded that a minimum of 1,000 cars be generally available, the 302 engine formed the basis of the Z-28 option, which could be ordered through any Chevrolet dealer. This was the most performance-oriented Camaro ever; and although in later years the designation was used again to signify so-called "sport" packages, that was little more than a marketing ploy: there was only one genuine Z-28.

OVERLEAF, RIGHT *By the late seventies the Camaro shape had gradually changed, but the options were still there . . .*

OVERLEAF, LEFT *1968 Camaro Z-28, with the kind of pipes so popular – and often so criticized – at the time.*

Its true status as a roadable race car for homologation purposes is easily seen in the sales charts. In 1967, its launch year, almost three-quarters of the 220,917 Camaros sold had a V8 powerplant and the rest were sixes. And the bulk of the V8 cars were 327 or 350 versions; just 602 had the competition-oriented 302 powerpack. Not even the name was a marketing tool; it really was box Z-28 that brought the 302 with all the racing parts, and the marketing teams picked the name up from there rather than the other way round.

Even in 1967, at the height of muscle power, the base Camaro was something of a plodder; its 155hp straight six gave it a top speed of only 104mph (166km/h). To get anything approaching real performance you had to go for the exclusive powerplant of the SS350, which gave 120mph (192km/h) flat out, and ran the quarter-mile at 15.8/89mph (142km/h).

Going the next step, to the 302, you were going All The Way. Vince Piggins had been involved in just about every performance application of the smallblock V8 from Corvette through Scarab, Chaparral and Penske, and he knew what few GM engineers knew – how to design an engine for the extremely tough world of competitive racing. His 302 used the 327 block with a forged steel crank out of the 283 and a racing-profile, long-

duration camshaft, all topped off with a giant 800cfm four-barrel Holley.

The handling package, which was mandatory with the engine option, included a limited-slip diff, a range of final drive ratios, heavy-duty suspension and the competition-tested power brakes with heavy-duty front discs and metallic rear linings. After that, there was still another long and tempting list of options, which included useful items like a close-ratio Muncie box or tuned headers.

There was even a choice of two cams, although one of them was clearly a race-only option, since it did nothing under 4,000rpm and was useless for any road-going application. Even without the red-hot cam, an out-of-the-box 302 with nothing better than a blueprint could reach close to 400hp, even though Chevrolet officially rated it at only 290hp, achieved at a mere 5800rpm.

The general opinion was that Chevrolet was only telling part of the story. The 302 revved happily up to 7,500rpm, although the clutch could only cope with about 7,000, and most people believed that while 290hp at 5,800 may have been correct, 350hp at 6200rpm was probably closer to the truth and was a far more reliable indication of the engine's true character. Most

road-going drivers will never hear an engine hit 7,000rpm in their lives, none that survive anyway.

Unsurprisingly, on the road the Z-28 was usually difficult to handle, idled roughly, rumbled once it was rolling and was very, very quick; 140mph (224km/h)-plus was a realistic top speed, as were 14-second quarters. There can be no doubt at all that the first Z-28 was a race car, but if any still existed, the proof came on the track. Right after its introduction the Z-28 beat the Mustangs, coming first and second in the Trans Am class of the 1968 Sebring 12-hour. It was class champion in the 1968 Trans Am series, and again in 1969, when it won 18 out of 25 races.

And those race wins certainly helped it to sell; after 602 sales in 1967, the GM "Mean Streak", as it was marketed, sold 7,199 units in 1968 and 19,000 in 1969, although by that time the real racing hard parts were getting harder and harder to find.

The 302 was GM's race-car version of the Camaro. In later years, when the horsepower event was at its zenith, Shelby took the ponycar element by storm with the stupendous GT 500. Chevrolet's best answer was the old 396 big-block, but a California dealership sold Camaro with the 425hp Corvette 427 motor. Sold as a conversion on the SS 350, the Dana Camaro had the big-block, Muncie four-speed, Positraction rearend, metallic brakes, tuned headers, heavy-duty clutch with NHRA scattershield and some extra instrumentation.

With all that on board, it still came out slower than the high-revving 302, with a top speed of just 130mph (208km/h). Acceleration was on a par, but with the extra weight up front the handling was measurably worse. The heavy engine made the car understeer, and even the beefed-up SS suspension package made little impression.

While the Chevrolet engineers were experimenting with racing through the 1960s Chevrolet's own performance options for Camaro were easy enough to get hold of; you could buy any race part in production in any of Chevy's 6,000 American dealerships almost as soon as it had proved its worth on a racetrack. When the racing experiments stopped, the parts dried up. Camaro soon became another gutless but de-smogged wonder, waiting for the engine technology to catch up with the twin demands of more power and clean air. In 1985, the Z-28 was replaced by the IROC-Z, using the glamor generated by the IROC series. But it's still no real successor to the 302 Z-28, developing only slightly more power than the road-going Z-28 of 1967.

MERCURY COUGAR

PRODUCTION SPAN
1967–72

ENGINE
90-degree Y-block V8 ohv

CAPACITY
4735cc/289ci
6390cc/390ci
5751cc/351ci
6997cc/427ci
7013cc/428ci

MAXIMUM POWER
289ci/200bhp
390ci/320/325bhp
351ci/250/300bhp
427ci/390bhp
428ci/335bhp
390ci/265/335bhp

CHASSIS/SUSPENSION
Unibody construction,
independent front
suspension by coil springs
and wishbones, rear
suspension by semi-elliptic
leaf springs

BODY STYLE
Four/five-seat saloon and
convertible

TOP SPEED
Variable: 390ci Cyclone GT
max speed 120mph
428ci Cyclone CJ 0–60mph
in 5.5 seconds

As the up-market division of Ford, Lincoln Mercury traditionally produced cars that were bigger and heavier (and more expensive) versions of Ford's best-sellers. Despite their size increase, performance options were still offered in the Lincoln Mercury range – the Comet, Mercury's version of Falcon, had a sports version in the Comet S-22 (which was later renamed Cyclone and then Cyclone GT), so it was natural there should be a Mustang variant in the Lincoln Mercury line-up.

This was intended to come in above Mustang but below the luxurious "personal car" that T-Bird had earlier become, and it was christened Mercury Cougar. With a 111in (282cm) wheelbase, it was three inches longer than Mustang, but the two were almost identical under the skin. Outside they were quite different; Cougar was good looking in its own right: it retained the long hood and short deck, but had sleek, smooth styling with concealed headlights. The suspension was changed to give a softer ride, and extra sound insulation removed the musclecar rumble from the interior. Cougar's base engine was

BOTTOM The Cougar, from Ford's upmarket Lincoln-Mercury Division, was intended as a "stretched" luxury version of Mustang.

BELOW The Ford hood badge on later Cougars displayed the company's involvement in racing.

LEFT The discreet hood ornament of the later, heavier Mercury Cougars.

the 200hp 289 V8, and went up through the V8 range to the Cougar GT package, which brought a 390 V8, revised suspension wide tires and wheels, and power brakes (with front discs). The extra weight all this added took something away in performance terms, but Cougar was, for all that, a pleasant enough sporting car.

But there was a still more luxurious package that saw Cougar fitted with air shocks, special wheel covers, luggage carrier, ski carrier, CB radio and even a 9in (23cm) TV. The real performance Cougar was the XR-7, intended as a competitor to the European imports. Its instruments were set in a walnut dash, and it had leather upholstery and an overhead console with map lights built in. Later still came an even more up-market version, the Dan Gurney Mercury Cougar Special, with special wheel trims, a chrome engine dress-up kit and a Dan Gurney signature decal.

The Cougar had its own performance options as well, and in addition many of the Mustang hard parts could be fitted to the

Cougar. With the factory-installed Handling Package (high-rate springs, heavy-duty shock absorbers, large-diameter sway bar, fast-rate steering, and wide tires and wheels), Cougar could be quite a performer in its own right, and in fact was voted *Motor Trend's* Car of the Year 1967. But Cougar was late into the muscle market and by 1968, its second year, emission controls were becoming compulsory, low-compression ratios and catalytic converters a foreseeable certainty.

But the next Cougar was the very rapid and powerful GT-E, with a detuned version of the famous 427 crossbolt engine giving 390hp: enough for it to be among the fastest of the pony-cars ever made. Later that year the GT-E swapped the 427 for the lower-rated 428 Cobra Jet, which gave 335hp.

But the performance versions were low-volume cars: only 602 GT-E Cougars were sold in the first year, and they were soon dropped from the range. Among a proliferation of engine options, Ford tried hard to promote Cougar through the "Eliminator" – a 428 Cougar with trick paint, sold in 1969 and '70, and dropped in 1971. It kept Cougar sales up for two seasons, though, along with the 351 Windsor engine; but despite a major face-lift for 1970, Cougar was competing in a declining market. Within another year or so it had vanished altogether, and the phenomenon of the musclecar was just a memory.

ABOVE *V8 engine of the original 1967 Mercury Cougar.*

LEFT *The Eliminator was sold during '69, '70 and '71, another tail-ender in the musclecar stakes and soon to be replaced by larger, overweight cars with no sporting pretensions at all.*

AMC JAVELIN

PRODUCTION SPAN
1968–1971

ENGINE
6-cyl ohv in-line
90-degree V8 ohv

CAPACITY
L6 3801cc/232ci
V8 4752cc/290ci
V8 5620cc/343ci
V8 6390cc/390ci
V8 5899cc/360ci

MAXIMUM POWER
323ci/145bhp
290ci/225/200bhp
343ci/280bhp
390ci/315bhp
360ci/245bhp

CHASSIS/SUSPENSION
Unibody construction, independent front suspension by coil spring/ wishbones, rear suspension by semi-elliptic leaf spring

BODY STYLE
Four-seat sports coupe

TOP SPEED
Variable. L6 max speed approx 80mph
289 V8 approx 100mph
Later big-block engines could attain 0–100mph in 16/17 seconds

Kenosha, Wisconsin, is the unlikely home of one of the big names in the sixties performance boom – a car born from the marriage of Nash, Rambler and Hudson.

In 1957 Rambler had released a 250ci, V8-engined Rebel, giving 190hp at 4900rpm. Later it got a 225hp version, but the performance and the sports car market were beyond AMC's usual boundary. The Rebel was soon dropped, but when Mustang appeared in 1965, AMC responded with the Marlin – a styling exercise based on the Rambler Classic. Though it looked the part, the performance wasn't there, and AMC remained firmly outside the muscle league dominated by Detroit's Big Three. Later came the 343ci Typhoon, added to a sporting lineup which by now included Marlin and Rebel.

Along with them came the ever-popular performance options, including a high-lift, long-duration cam, competition lifters and heavy-duty valve springs, a 4.44:1 rear axle and a cold-air system. But even this was only a small step, and the AMC operation was not as sophisticated as its competitors. The obvious move was to follow the lead of the other makers, and soon AMC put a big V8 into a much smaller car, the Rambler Rogue (the smallest car in the AMC lineup). Even then its performance was less than startling, with a 20-second 0-100mph time and slow quarter-mile times. The Rogue was still not the car to lift AMC into the big league.

The car that did was announced in the fall of 1967 – the Javelin. Better-looking than Marlin, it had Mustang ponycar looks, with long hood and short deck. As the Javelin SST it had the 343ci, 280hp V8, which placed it right between the highest and the lowest of Mustang outputs and almost exactly matched the 295hp 350 smallblock in Camaro and Nova.

Javelin ran 100mph (160km/h) in 17 seconds, even with some strangely gentle gear ratios; all the testers of the time found them close, and got better acceleration by starting from the line in second. But the consensus was in favor of Javelin; it was better than Marlin and sold better to prove it – 56,000 units in the first year, outselling Marlin by more than ten times. Flushed with success, AMC introduced a smaller, two-seat version midway through the following year, and called it AMX.

AMC described the car as a "Walter Mitty Ferrari", and aimed it at a low-volume run, placed between the imports and domestic ponycars. But it was never sold as planned – 20,000 in three years, compared to the 20,000 per year AMC were looking for – and was never as well liked as the Javelin. Which is a pity; it was fast, with its 390ci, 315hp V8: 0-100mph in 16 was realistic, and quarters in low 14s high 90s. But it was also heavy, at 3,200lbs (1,440kg), and needed the heavy-duty suspension, with a big front sway bar included, as a mandatory option.

The Javelins went well on the racetrack, especially in the Trans Am series, turning in 0-60 (0-967km) in less than 5 seconds, and topping out at around 175mph (280km/h). But AMC still lacked the corporate muscle to back up its street muscle; still it opened 1970 with The Machine. This was basically a Rebel two-door hardtop, plus the braking and suspension kits and the 390in (990cm) V8 giving 340hp and some very respectable performance. But by this time peformance was a dirty word in Detroit; just as AMC finally got their act together and developed a car that was demonstrably a competitor in the muscle stakes, it all came crashing down around their ears.

SHELBY COBRA

PRODUCTION SPAN

1962–1968

ENGINE

90-degree V8

CAPACITY

4260cc/260ci
4735cc/289ci
6997cc/427ci

MAXIMUM POWER

260ci/164bhp
289ci/up to 271bhp
427ci/485bhp

CHASSIS/SUSPENSION

Tubular steel frame;
transverse leaf spring
suspension replaced from
1965 by independent
suspension with coil springs
and wishbones

BODY STYLE

Open two-seater

TOP SPEED

427ci versions, 0–60mph in
3.8 seconds, maximum
speed 162mph

In October 1963 a new American sports car made its race debut at Riverside, and in the hands of Billy Krause the red-painted two-seater established a massive supremacy (and a lead of one-and-a-half miles over the rest of the pack) before a stub axle failure put it out of the race. It was an unfortunate way to retire after such an auspicious beginning, but nevertheless the message was loud and clear: from now on, Cobra was a name to be reckoned with. Over the next three years it proved the point absolutely, and dominated virtually every kind of motor race.

Texan Carroll Hall Shelby had been a successful race driver until a heart condition prompted his retirement. By sheer co-incidence, Shelby had driven the Ulster TT in the same Porsche Speedster that Zora Duntov had piloted around Le Mans before going to work for GM – mostly on Corvette.

There was, in the early 1950s, a rash of small American sports cars aimed at matching the European mastery of the road-racing technique. Many had tried – Reventlow, Scarab, Devin, Bocar – but only Briggs Cunningham achieved fame at it, although Scarab was a name to be reckoned with. Shelby was the man who hit upon the perfect answer. His proposal to marry an American V8 with a European chassis was considered by GM but rejected. The racing connotation was too overt, and in any case GM had its own arrangements with Jim Hall's Chaparral, Roger Penske and Smokey Yunick. And in road terms, GM thought that Corvette was already the car Shelby wanted to build.

Shelby went to Ford next, and his idea of putting its new smallblock 221 V8 into an aluminum-bodied chassis from small specialist car builders AC, at Thames Ditton, England, arrived at the very moment Lee Iacocca was preparing Ford's Total Performance crusade, which was launched in 1963. From that moment on, the Shelby/Iacocca team established a rapport that continued to generate both success and excitement right into the late 1980s.

Ford gave an emphatic go-ahead, and work on a first proto-type began in the California workshop Shelby shared with customizer and drag racer Dean Moon. The body, made from folded sheet metal, was a basic open two-seater with a rudi-mentary cockpit behind a long aggressive hood. That first car worked hard for its living; painted a different color each time, it

Originally just a basic racing car, now a desirable (and expensive) collector's piece, the phenomenal 427 Cobra. The 90 degree V8 engine delivered tremendous power, particularly in its bigblock 427ci guise.

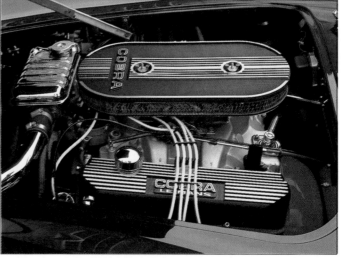

"A Cobra", said one journalist, "is just a race car with enough legality built in so you can drive it on the street."

was sent out on road test after road test, and appeared on several magazine covers looking like a different car on each one. Soon there were buyers lining up for a sports car they imagined was already in mass-production.

But it wasn't then, and nor was it at any time in the future. Each car was carefully built up by hand, each was different from the cars ahead of and behind it on the assembly line. This dedicated philosophy of manufacture was a source of constant problems to the Ford accountants in later years when the Mustang was added to the Shelby repertoire. To begin with,

though, it worked fine on the small sports car. As improvements or modifications were conceived they were just built into the next car down the line and all those following; the idea of waiting for the next season to make the changes somehow never gained much credibility with Shelby. The result was that no two cars are exactly alike, a situation complicated by the fact that many owners would hear of a new modification and bring their car back to the factory to have it altered.

Shelby, Ford and the USA their first ever World Manufacturer's Championship, beating Il Commendatore – and everyone else – at Daytona, Sebring, Oulton Park, Nurburgring, Rossfeld, Rheims and, rubbing salt in it, at Ferrari's home track, Monza. The only upset in this glorious series was Le Mans, the one occasion when the Cobra followed Ferrari across the finish line.

That result could well have gone the other way if the Cobras had used Ford's new big-block 7-liter engine. On top of the extra chassis tuning work needed to handle the extra weight (never mind a power output that would have given the Cobra a 250mph (400km/h) top speed potential), there was a political backdrop to consider as well. Ford had at last produced its GT40, and although all the potential was there it seemed that early teething problems were preventing the factory team from showing too well in 1965. Shelby could have been in a difficult position if he'd done better than the factory with its own engine – especially on the same racetrack. The following season, of course, the GT40 returned to Le Mans with the added touch of Shelby magic. Its 1-2-3-4 win in 1966 was followed by more wins in '67, '68 and '69.

Back in the USA the Cobra continued to win – to such an extent that drag-racing rules were changed to keep it out. In November 1965 Craig Breedlove took a Cobra to Bonneville and grabbed 23 national and international records. On the street, the Cobra established a reputation for sports car performance and handling that has since become *the* benchmark to which all others are compared. As the only sports car with supercar performance ever made, Cobra still waits for its position at the top of the pile to be usurped.

And that's in no small way due to the eventual adoption of the 427 engine, although only a handful were made. From a total of 1011 Cobras ever built, just 356 were the big-block version. With a performance curve that's more of a straight line – going up – the 427 Cobra had 485 horsepower under its hood and hit 60mph (96km/h) from rest in a staggering 4.5 seconds. In race tune the 0-60 time dropped to 3.8 seconds. 100mph (160km/h) came up in 8.6 seconds, and the Cobra turned in a phenomenal 0-100mph (160km/h) and stop in 14 seconds! With a top speed of 162mph (259km/h) the "base" 427 in street trim outstripped the performance of most modern supercars.

Its astounding performance was matched in the press by equally astounding road tests. The motoring journalists of the day reported back. "It's only fair to warn you that out of the 300 guys who switched to the 427 Cobra only two went back to women ... unless you own real estate near the Bonneville salt flats you'll never see the top end ... a Cobra is a race car with enough legality built into it so you can drive it on the street ... I bought the 427 from Shelby on the spot and gave a check, using my driver's license for identification. We both realized that it might be the last time either of us would see the document."

In 1965, with the FIA GT Championship secure, Shelby withdrew the Cobras from competition, and concentrated on the GT40. Off the track, his attention was being taken by Ford's new musclecar, and soon the Shelby magic would transform the Mustang.

This was especially true in the case of engines; the first 75 cars were given a 221 smallblock V8 overbored to a healthier 260ci. But when Ford upped the stock block to 289in (734cm) and Shelby adopted it, there was a queue of owners waiting to have their existing 260 replaced by the larger powerplant.

After that first race appearance at Riverside, the Cobra reigned supreme on the racetrack and off it; the only thing it hadn't done so far was to realize Shelby's personal ambition, which was to "blow Ferrari off the track" (or words to that effect!) In 1965 that dream was realized as well. Cobra brought

CORVETTE GRAND SPORT

PRODUCTION SPAN
1963

ENGINE
90-degree all aluminum V8

CAPACITY
6177cc/377ci

MAXIMUM POWER
485bhp @ 6000rpm

CHASSIS/SUSPENSION
Hand-made tubular ladder frame; independent front suspension by coil springs and wishbones; Corvette independent rear suspension with transverse leaf spring

BODY STYLE
Two-seat sports coupe or open two-seater

TOP SPEED
Dependent on trim/gear ratios. 0–100mph in 9 seconds, top speed in excess of 150mph

In 1957, the AMA formulated a resolution that was an effective ban on manufacturer involvement in motor sport. All of Detroit's Big Three were party to the resolution although it obviously suited the smaller signatories (including several truck makers) rather better than it did the big corporations. Over the course of the next few years both Ford and GM failed to abide by the letter of that ruling; Ford abandoned it completely with the declaration of its "Total Performance" program in 1963; GM upheld the spirit of it at least.

When news of the Shelby Cobra got out, there were those at GM – Zora Duntov especially – who felt the need to compete. When Billy Krause and his Cobra trounced the GM cars at Riverside in late 1962, the Chevrolet engineers knew that the new Corvette Sting Ray, which was already in the works for the 1963 model year, was outclassed and outgunned by the lightweight two-seater from Dearborn. But honor demanded they put up a fight, and in fact the plans to build a new and far lighter Corvette had been sanctioned by Chevrolet boss Simon "Bunkie" Knudsen back in the summer of 1962. Under the heading "Operation Mongoose", Knudsen approved the building of what could have been the most devastating GM product ever – Corvette Grand Sport.

FIA rules demanded that at least 100 similar cars be built and offered for sale for them to be eligible for racing; the Chevrolet plan was to build 125, keeping 25 back for the factory and leaving 100 others for private racers to buy. The 25 cars in the "works" team would be built in-house; manufacture of the others would be by outside shops. Chevrolet was on good terms with Roger Penske, Smokey Yunick and, of course, Jim Hall's Chaparral team.

But GM management, determined to live up to the AMA resolution and highly embarrassed by the high profile its errant racers at Chevrolet were adopting, acted to prevent their plans – aimed long-term at the winner's circle at Le Mans. In January 1963, Chairman Frederic Donner wrote a memo to all his staff stating quite clearly that the company was and would remain a party to the AMA resolution, and that all unofficial racing and performance programs had to stop.

Production had already begun on the first five vehicles, and although much of the chassis development work was already finished, the design work on the new engine, which Duntov knew the race car would need to compete against the Cobra, was axed. What was left was a ladder-type frame bearing which bore little resemblance to the stock Sting Ray item. Large-diameter side rails were joined by cross members, and a huge kick-up raised each end to accommodate the suspension.

Although the frame was new, the suspension was basically that of the production Sting Ray treated to a massive weight-saving program. Where new lightweight alloys were unavailable, unsuitable or uneconomic, the existing steel items were machined and drilled to save the last possible pound of weight. With the new Independent Rear Suspension introducd for 1963 production came the four-wheel discs that would make it to the line in 1964; at this time they were only just workable on the new super-light race car and completely underpowered for the street cars.

The body was still fiberglass, but hand-laid, extremely thin and very light. It followed the lines of the new-for-1963

production cars, although it went without the controversial (but now highly admired) rear window divider and had fixed lights behind Plexiglas in place of the rotating production lights. The mechanism needed to operate them included two electric motors and weighed in far too heavily for racing. The race car had stock instruments with a revised version of stock steering.

With aerodynamics still in its infancy, the race car had a fairly high drag factor and suffered even worse from aerodynamic lift – a component of road and race car design then hardly appreciated, never mind understood. The lift was so bad that the cars had constant problems as the hoods were blown up in the driver's face at speed. The new and now-canceled race engine was intended to overcome the poor drag factor; but with that program canceled there was only a more or less stock-injected engine with experimental aluminum heads available.

Zora Duntov took the car to Sebring in December 1962, for a tire-testing session; the public attention these sessions received was largely responsible for Donner's cancellation memo. The engines that never saw the light of day, though they would have suffered the short lifespan of all aluminum racetrack screamers, could have been a Corvette legend in their own right.

They were based on the 327 V8, cast in aluminum and using the stock bottom end. Duntov – who'd already shown this skill with Ford's flathead V8 – designed a new "semi-hemi" cylinder head to allow large-diameter valves. Following in the footsteps of his "ARDUN" conversion on the Ford, the valves lifted high and stayed open long, lifting power high in the rev range. In theory the 16-plug engine was good for about 600hp. Without this, though, the Grand Sport Corvettes gained only standard 360hp fuel-injection iron engines.

The Donner memo stopped Chevrolet from racing. Close study revealed that it did not prohibit the Corvette Grand Sport from going to the track. The Corvette group arranged for three of the cars to be "loaned" to favored racers – Dick Doane and Grady Davis. For the first part of 1963, the Grand Sports appeared at a variety of events and their teething problems were gradually ironed out. Class wins became more and more frequent, and then came the first outright win at Watkins Glen in August.

But it was later in the year that the Grand Sport achieved its ambition – wiping out the Cobras. In the hands of the Mecom race team, three blue-liveried Grand Sports were among the massive Chevrolet-powered contingent which shipped out to Nassau for the Speed Week that December. A Chevrolet engineer at the time, Paul Van Valkenburg, recalls that Shelby "almost fell off the pier" when he saw what amounted to a full-house Chevrolet works team showing up for the boat.

Mecom had both the cars that had been running through the 1963 season, plus the third finished car that somehow got out of the factory without being spotted, and he had three very special engines. They were 377in (956cm) aluminum engines, with aluminum heads and four dual-choke Weber carburetors, good for 485hp. Along with the hardware, Mecom and the other teams running Chevrolet power had the benefit of almost every Chevrolet engineer on the payroll, all of whom had

strangely decided to vacation in the same place at the same time.

Their presence paid off; when the Grand Sports had a differential problem, it was quickly traced to the use of new "stiff" parts, and a solution found. After that it was Chevrolet benefit week in Nassau. As one contemporary writer observed, "They won everything but the Grand Priz of Volkswagens." In the Governor's Cup race, the Grand Sports finished in third, fourth and fifth; the nearest Cobra was eighth. In the Nassau Trophy, the problem of airflow lifting the hood left the two Grand Sports entered in fourth and eighth place after frequent stops to have the hoods taped closed. The first Cobra home

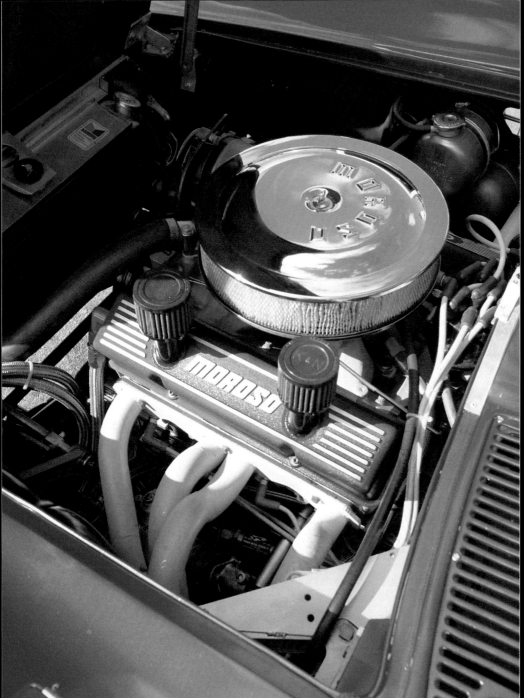

came in seventh.

Although the Corvette group had good reason to be pleased with itself, its joy was short-lived. Back at Warren, Michigan, plans for Daytona were underway, and the two remaining Grand Sports out of the total of five that were built were being cut down into roadster configuration. But the success at Nassau had once again attracted too much attention, and newspaper talk of a Chevrolet Race Team once again prompted Frederic Donner to call his would-be racers at Chevrolet to order.

This time he was serious, and all racing hardware had to be shipped out of the plant immediately. By the same process of cooperation that had seen so many race teams compete successfully with Chevrolet engines and Chevrolet products, the spare cars went to good homes. They appeared in various guises and with varying degrees of success all through 1964, and in December Roger Penske went back to Nassau. With no help from Detroit, he faced one of the earliest 427 Shelby Cobras and Ford's new GT40 – and beat both of them, winning three of the major events.

The Grand Sports survive in various forms, and Mike Begley's immaculately restored coupe went back to Nassau again in 1984, 21 years after its triumph. Its appearance there is a small and sad reminder of what could have been if the enthusiasts at Chevrolet had won out over the hard-nosed accountants.

SHELBY MUSTANG

PRODUCTION SPAN

1966–1970

ENGINE

90-degree V8

CAPACITY

4735cc/289ci
6390cc/390ci
5751cc/351ci
7013cc/428ci

MAXIMUM POWER

289ci/306bhp
390ci/335bhp
351ci/290bhp
427ci/390bhp
428ci/400bhp

CHASSIS/SUSPENSION

Tubular steel frame.
Transverse leaf spring
suspension replaced from
1965 by independent
suspension with coil springs
and wishbones

BODY STYLE

Four-seat sports coupe

TOP SPEED

427ci versions, 0–60mph in
3.8 seconds, maximum
speed 162mph

After the astounding success of the Cobra, and the immeasurable good publicity it achieved for Ford under its Total Performance banner, it was only natural that the partnership with Shelby should be extended to include an ultra-high-performance version of the Mustang. The move towards road vehicle involvement had come in 1964; from then on Ford had been advertising "Doctor" Shelby's Cobra Tonic, a "marvellous elixir for Fairlanes, Falcons and Galaxies, in ten strengths up to 343hp." And, of course, the Cobra was available for street use as well as racing, establishing an unparalleled reputation for performance and handling.

Ford's commitment to Total Performance as a sales tool was absolute. Lee Iacocca fully believed the "Race on Sunday, sell on Monday" adage, and applied it vigorously to the Mustang – although as Detroit's most successful first-year model of the decade, Mustang hardly needed any help. Named, according to Shelby, because the distance from the engine shop to the final assembly line was "about" 350ft, the GT350 was as purebred a race car as the Cobra, and was a long way from being a dressed-up production Mustang.

Like Cobra, it was designed without compromise, was built on an individual basis, and once again almost all of the first year's production of 562 were different. The Shelby policy of incorporating modifications and improvements as soon as they were finalized was also adopted, and the converse was also true: if they ran short of any particular part, then the cars were built without it until further supplies arrived. The result, once again, was that no two GT350 Mustangs were the same as each other in every respect.

In fact, the first big change came after only 250 cars had been built. Though the Shelby Mustangs were formidable street cars, they made no profit for Ford, and the accountants descended on Shelby to put his house in order for him. They made a number of changes on the production lines that Shelby didn't like, but which did add to the car's appeal. Then Hertz bought a quantity to add to its rental fleet, making the GT350H available to members of the Hertz Sports Car Club. From then on the GT350H began to appear at every drag strip in the United States, and the tales of cars returned to the rental lot on Monday with burn marks where an NHRA roll cage had been welded in and removed are legion.

When the Mustang faced competition from Camaro and Firebird (among others) in 1967 Ford responded with a mid-term face-lift that made it a bigger and heavier car. It had the desired effect on sales of the "ordinary" Mustang, but presented the GT350 concept with one or two problems. A fiberglass front end reduced the weight of the new overhang, and the addition of convenience features like air-conditioning allowed the car to be positioned as a luxury GT, but the Shelby performance credentials were definitely compromised by the changes.

So in 1967 Shelby responded by switching to big-block power, and the massive 428ci engine became the performance powerpack in a new car – the GT500. This time the name was chosen simply because Shelby thought it was a good one; as much justification as there had been for naming the original the GT350. With air-conditioning, power steering and even automatic gearbox, the GT500 was far more civilized and

The larger and heavier second-generation version of Shelby's GT 350 was still a formidable street car.

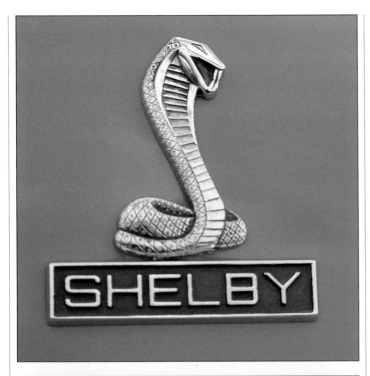

generally acceptable than the GT350, and sales increased accordingly. Furthermore, the GT500 packed an almost unbelievable performance punch.

It was widely said that a GT500 could destroy a set of rear tires in just one evening's street-racing; advertised as "the Road Cars," the GT500 became a feared opponent from Van Nuys in LA through Woodward in Detroit. But even those formidable street-fighters weren't the pinnacle of the Shelby Mustang's desirability. When the Cobra production ended in 1967 so that Ford could maximize the sales value of Shelby's work on Mustang, Shelby filled the gap in his own line-up with two of the most desirable cars ever – convertible versions of both the GT350 and 500.

Then in 1968 the GT350 got the new and more powerful 302 smallblock, followed in 1969 by the 351 Windsor engine – added along with more fiberglass panels in response to the weight added by Mustang's 1969 restyle. Midway through 1969 came the 500KR King of the Road, using Ford's 428 Cobra-Jet engine, and this became the standard GT500 powerplant from then on. To be fair, there wasn't much further to go anyway. Ford itself was now in direct competition with Shelby through its own Mustang variants, the Boss 302, the Boss 429 and the Mach 1; there was a big-block Corvette and performance variants of the GM Camaro/Firebird clone, and there was also an air of change in the wind.

For some time the high-performance musclecars like the Shelbys had been hard to insure. With a horrifying accident rate which was a direct result of a performance capability well beyond most people's driving capabilities, the Shelbys vied with the Plymouth Superbird and Dodge Daytona Charger for the dubious honor of being the most crashed car in the history of the auto industry. And as a Federal ban on horsepower advertising approached, Shelby saw the change that was coming and asked Ford to release him from the Total Performance program. There were just 601 Shelby Mustangs completed at the time; they were given air dams, black hood stripes and 1970 serial numbers and were the last of the 14,368 Mustangs Shelby built; the days of legend were over.

PONTIAC
TRANS AM

PRODUCTION SPAN

1969 to date

ENGINE

6-cyl ohv in-line
90-degree V8

CAPACITY

L6 4735cc/250ci
V8 5735cc/350ci
V8 6554cc/400ci

MAXIMUM POWER

250ci/175/230bhp
350ci/265–330bhp
400ci/330/335/345bhp

CHASSIS/SUSPENSION

Unibody construction;
independent front
suspension by coil springs
and wishbones; rear
suspension by semi-elliptic
leaf springs

BODY STYLE

Four-seat sports coupe

TOP SPEED

Variable according to
engine/tune

By the late 1960s the muscle boom in Detroit was over, or at least it should have been. But then Pontiac announced – very quietly – the Trans Am option for Firebird. This seemed to be just a cosmetic package for Firebird 400, and there was no hint that this car was meant to replace the two-seater Pontiac had been hoping to build instead of the Camaro F-car it was forced to adopt. Even its name – taken from the SCCA series in which Chevrolet's thinly disguised Z-28 had reigned supreme for three seasons – alerted GM to the true nature of the beast Pontiac had created.

The fact that the 400in (1,016cm) engine was beyond the Trans Am series capacity limit may have helped with the camouflage, but a 303 tunnel-port engine was already under development – though, sadly, it never made production. The Trans Am was seen at Pontiac much as the GTO had been almost ten years before. So in proper muscle tradition, Trans Am was not a car, but an option package. With the base car you had to order the Ram Air engine plus front discs, variable ratio power steering and a limited-slip rear end. The external option package included the Trans Am hood, front air dam, rear wing, air extractors for the fenders, stiffer springs and shocks, and Fiberglass-belted tires.

There was no launch razzmatazz, and sales reflected its secretive debut exactly: only 689 – plus the only eight Trans Am convertibles ever made – were built. In 1970, although Trans Am remained a Firebird option, it was the top performance choice for Firebird buyers and brought a 345hp 400 V8 in response to the right checks in the option boxes. And better still, Trans Am was probably the first musclecar to have conquered the eternal ride/handling compromise that had left so many of its contemporaries lacking. It wasn't harsh, or bouncy, yet the suspension worked very well, to the point that *Hot Rod* magazine thought the handling was beyond the psychological limits of most of the people who would drive it.

Without the 303 homologate tunnel port, racing was held up; the SCCA refused to homologate the only 25 such engines in existence, so Trans Am raced with Chevy's 302; they couldn't even use the 1969 body, since SCCA rules called for 1,000, and they hadn't yet been built. During the season Firebird didn't

The original Firebird (below) was roughly the size and shape of the GTO. By 1983 it was changing into a sleeker, European-style sports car, and by 1988, as these pictures show, the process was complete.

win a single race, but placed third in the manufacturers' championship with 32 points.

For the 1970s, still haunted by the F-car clone forced on them in 1967, Pontiac insisted on full cooperation during design, to ensure that the new Firebirds would be as different from Camaro as possible. Chevrolet had started work on the follow-up to Camaro in 1966 – before the first one had been seen in public. Pontiac began work a year later, but its design was so good-looking it became the base for the second-generation F-car from both divisions.

Although the base engine was the Chevy straight six, the Trans Am had a 345hp V8; as *the* performance option, it was an image-builder for the rest of the range. It was also a homologation special aimed directly at the SCCA series. But the street car was too expensive, and Pontiac couldn't sell enough to get the certification; in 1970, it had to move 3,200 of them through the dealerships. Pontiac Chairman F James McDonald decided that it could be done; he instructed the sales force to do it. They did.

For 1971 the 345hp engine was no longer the top option; now there was a massive 455, rated at 370hp in Catalina, Bonneville and Grand Prix, but quoted at 335hp in Trans Am. Horsepower was definitely on the way out, compression ratios were down to 8:1, and all the musclecars were being robbed of their powers. Although ponycar sales – a sort of halfway house between family compacts and proper musclecars – had seen falling demand (and sales) since the Mustang's second year, the same was not true of the real performance cars. Demand was as high as ever, but legislation was in the wind. In 1972, horsepower advertising was banned, and Firebird practically vanished as well. Pontiac slipped from third place in the sales league and stayed down after a serious strike stopped Firebird and Camaro production. More than 1,000 cars waiting on the line had to be scrapped because they were too late to be 1972 models and illegal under 1973 regulations.

Within months the OPEC countries began to flex their new found muscles, and as far as Detroit was concerned, performance was over, at least for the next decade.

PLYMOUTH ROAD RUNNER SUPERBIRD

PRODUCTION SPAN
1970

ENGINE
90-degree V8 hemi

CAPACITY
6980cc/426ci

MAXIMUM POWER
425bhp

CHASSIS/SUSPENSION
Unibody construction; independent front suspension by coil springs and wishbones; rear suspension by semi-elliptic leaf springs

BODY STYLE
Four-seat sports saloon

TOP SPEED
Approx 200mph in race trim

In the late 1960s the musclecar era took a new and astounding twist as Plymouth – always one of the leading exponents of the musclecar art – used its dealer network to get NASCAR homologation for an all-out race car that was also available to the road-going public. The car was a modified version of the previous year's, although calling it modified hardly does justice to its outrageous appearance.

The science of vehicle aerodynamics was applied to the Roadrunner, and with swooping droop-snoot plastic nosecone and monstrous rear wing, the Plymouth Roadrunner Superbird was probably the most excessive vehicle of the entire sixties style phenomenon.

Plymouth performance went back to the 426 powerplant in the 1956 Fury and the company produced the Barracuda as its answer to Mustang. But already, in late 1963, Plymouth had put its "Orange Monster" into the musclecar arena. The "Monster" was not a car, but an engine: the astounding 426-111 Super Stock hemi which had, in one season of drag racing, brought the factory no less than 26 track records, and the 1962 NHRA Championship. With a useful 425hp at its command, the Orange Monster was the supreme drag-race powerplant of the season – and these hemi engines have a legendary reputation even now. Away from the drag strip, the Monster was the talking

Its dramatic aerodynamics marked the SuperBird out as something special. With 426 hemi it reached around 200mph in race trim.

point of the NASCAR circuits, to which Plymouth was heavily committed, and it pulled off a 1-2-3 win at Daytona in 1964.

Within a year the hemi was out on the street in the Belvedere, now a five-seat family sedan with 425hp available. The next step for Belvedere was the Satellite, and among its engine choices was the 426 hemi engine. By careful consideration of the order blank, and checks in the right boxes, a dedicated racer could order what amounted to a ready-to-race NASCAR winner straight off the showroom floor. Richard Petty proved it by winning the 1967 NASCAR Championship with one in 1967.

In 1968 the hemi was offered exclusively on the new GTX,

and a sixties street-racing legend was born. The Belvedere first had become the Belvedere GTX, then the GTX and finally the GTX Road Runner, soon to be just the Roadrunner. In its first year there was a choice of two body styles, each with dummy hood scoops, special wheels, Road Runner nameplates and a decal of the cartoon bird of the same name on the sides and rear. There was a choice of engines as well – either the small-block 383 (with manifolds and heads from the 440) or the real thing, the 426 hemi.

Motor Trend magazine immediately voted it their Car of the Year 1968, and said it was "the simplest, starkest, most brazenly pure, non-compromising super car in history". And they were

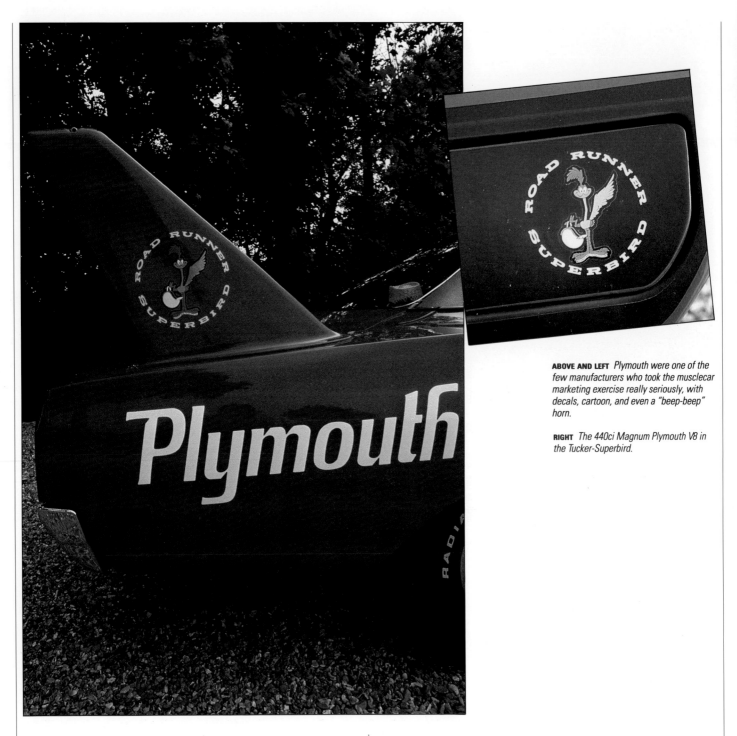

ABOVE AND LEFT *Plymouth were one of the few manufacturers who took the musclecar marketing exercise really seriously, with decals, cartoon, and even a "beep-beep" horn.*

RIGHT *The 440ci Magnum Plymouth V8 in the Tucker-Superbird.*

testing the 383, never mind the real killer.

For the Road Runner GTX, Plymouth adopted an unusual attitude, building a car for the job in hand rather than to a price, the opposite of the way most cars were (and still are) designed and built. It left all comfort and convenience items out of the car, in favor of performance hard parts, and the technique worked. The 383 had a sticker price only a few hundred dollars above the market rate; it was also a lot of car for the money, though, so the equation balanced well.

The extra money paid for the 383 engine, a handling package with anti-sway bar, heavy-duty shocks, torsion bar and heavy rear leaf springs. Even so – and with its wide tires – the car weighed in at 3660lbs (1,647kg) and could travel at frightening speeds. It was fine on the track, but a dangerous blend for a road-going car.

In 1969 the dummy hood scoops became a real cold-air induction system called Coyote Duster, but the big change came in 1970, when Plymouth launched the final member of the "Rapid Transit System", as its performance-car inventory was called. Along with everything else about the car, the name was outrageously ostentatious: the Roadrunner Superbird. It was designed specifically for the 200mph (320km/h) NASCAR speedways, and dual quad carbs gave the 426 hemi 425hp. With aerodynamic droop-snoot, pop-up headlights and a huge rear wing, the 1,920 examples built were offered to the public for one year only. It was a sell-out.

DODGE
DAYTONA
CHARGER

PRODUCTION SPAN
1969

ENGINE
90-degree V8 hemi

CAPACITY
6980cc/426ci

MAXIMUM POWER
425bhp

CHASSIS/SUSPENSION
Unibody construction;
independent front
suspension by coil springs
and wishbones; rear
suspension by semi-elliptic
leaf springs

BODY STYLE
Four-seat sports saloon

TOP SPEED
Approx 200mph in race
trim

RIGHT AND BELOW RIGHT *The Charge.*
one of the first Detroit cars to benefit .
the application of aerodynamics, and was
about 20 per cent faster as a result.

Plymouth and Dodge development run more or less parallel, especially when it comes to the low-volume specialist cars. In the sixties, the Scat Pack was the Dodge equivalent of Plymouth's Rapid Transit System, and although Dodge didn't embrace the marketing techniques of the era as readily as Plymouth, there were still cars like the Super Bee and the rest of the similarly named range – all with relevant striping.

The Dart was the Dodge equivalent of Plymouth's Mustang-basher, the Barracuda, and was the tidiest of what Dodge eventually called the "Scat Pack". Like the Barracuda, Dart developed as the musclecar era became more and more performance-oriented.

The fabled 425hp hemi engine had a part in the Dodge story too. Named the Orange Monster, it powered Dodge and Plymouth to a seemingly endless succession of victories in drag racing and NASCAR; it took the 1962 NHRA Championship under the hood of a Dodge and, mentioned earlier, was competitive enough to secure a 1-2-3 victory at Daytona in 1964, two seasons later.

On the street, the Dodge-badged hemi was the excellent 425hp Dodge Coronet, which was possibly one of the better vehicles of the whole musclecar era. The next step was the Dart GTS with the 375hp big-block 440 and a top speed above 120mph. It went 0-100mph in 15 seconds, which was no mean feat for any car 25 years ago. Adding the 426 hemi gave an extra 55hp, but it also added 150lbs (68kg) over the nose. The consequent handling disadvantage meant that it was offered as a race-only option.

Then in 1968 came a new Dodge, aimed directly at recapturing former glories at Daytona. The current race effort was based around the hemi-engined Charger, and while no extra power was available from the engine (within the rules) there was some advantage to be gained from the bodywork. The science of automobile aerodynamics was just coming of age, and for Dodge the first fruits came in the form of a new plastic nosecone concealing pop-up headlights and a massive rear wing. Mounted on the rear deck, it towered over the roofline and dominated the appearance of the car from any angle; a silhouette you just couldn't miss, or ignore.

Chevrolet and Chaparral had already discovered that a rear wing countered lift to such an extent that it loaded the suspension; their solution was to fix it directly to the wheel hub, but that was obviously not possible on something that had to be homologated as a production car. This car was designed for the NASCAR ovals, however, not for a road course, and the problem was nothing that couldn't be overcome. Especially as only 505 cars were built – just five more than were needed for homologation. The sticker price was $8,000; it began its series of race wins at Talladega.

Named the Dodge Daytona Charger, those startling aerodynamic tricks improved airflow over the car by some 20 per cent. In practical terms that meant a higher top speed, and the extra mph meant that the new aerodynamic car gained 500yds (450m) a lap over the previous car. Running alongside the Plymouth version (called Super Bird), the droop-snoot Charger dominated the 1970 NASCAR season, winning 38 out of

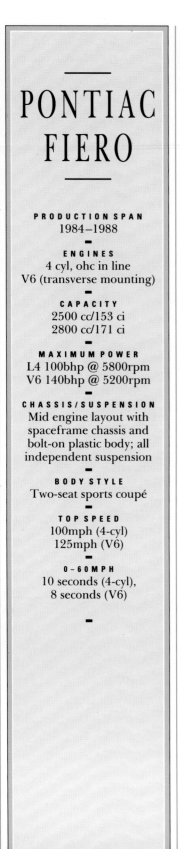

PONTIAC FIERO

PRODUCTION SPAN
1984–1988
▬
ENGINES
4 cyl, ohc in line
V6 (transverse mounting)
▬
CAPACITY
2500 cc/153 ci
2800 cc/171 ci
▬
MAXIMUM POWER
L4 100bhp @ 5800rpm
V6 140bhp @ 5200rpm
▬
CHASSIS/SUSPENSION
Mid engine layout with
spaceframe chassis and
bolt-on plastic body; all
independent suspension
▬
BODY STYLE
Two-seat sports coupé
▬
TOP SPEED
100mph (4-cyl)
125mph (V6)
▬
0-60MPH
10 seconds (4-cyl),
8 seconds (V6)
▬

When, after years of speculation, Fiero finally went public for the 1984 model year, Pontiac advertising claimed that it was one of the most innovative cars in American auto history. It was a bold statement from any manufacturer, but Fiero has largely managed to live up to it.

The most significant new feature was that except for Corvair, it was the first American sports car featuring the mid-engine layout which had been mandatory for European sports cars since the Miura in 1963; and there was more breakaway technology, making the Fiero a near-revolutionary two-seater. Interestingly, there was to be no corporate Fiero; other GM divisions do not make their own versions of it.

The Fiero began as a corporate project in the late seventies, in the Advanced and Experimental design studio. When initial engineering and chassis work was complete, the decision to go ahead was taken in 1979, and designers Irv Ribicki, Chuck Jordan and Dave Holles were set to work under the chief of the Advanced III studio, Ron Hill. It was only in April 1980, after the first full-size clay had been completed, that Fiero became a Pontiac project, passing into the hands of designer Jack Schinella at Pontiac II and chief engineer Hulki Aldikacti.

It was GM's first mid-engined car, their first spaceframe chassis, and featured bolt-on Endura plastic body panels, which absorb minor knocks and never rust. These plastic panels first appeared as nosecones and small body parts on cars like GTO, Trans Am and Firebird, and went on to wider usage throughout the industry. Fiero is the first GM car to use it as a complete body skinning, and this must have contributed to Fiero's success in winning an award from the Industrial Designers' Association, for innovation and styling.

At first Fiero had a rather slow 2.5 four-cylinder engine which could barely summon up more than 100hp but slung in the Fiero's lightweight spaceframe chassis it gave the two-seater a 0-60 time of about 10 seconds. The new V6 engines, however, were almost ready, and in its guise as the Indy Pace car, Fiero appeared with an aluminum V6 turbo which delivered some 350hp. Its track behaviour demonstrated quite clearly that the chassis was more than capable of handling the power, and the growing ranks of Fiero fans prepared for the moment when the imports – and perhaps even the home-grown Corvette – would be beaten on their own terms.

The threat to Corvette performance supremacy was real enough; the 84 Corvette was newly-released as GM's 25,000-dollar supercar and yet the cheaper plastic-bodied Fiero two-seater looked likely to give it a run for its money. Lacking the exotic digital technology of Corvette, the Fiero was still roomy enough, and comfortable enough, to take on Corvette as a carrier of people. One of the reasons for its appealing appearance is the fact that it is very low and very wide; inside, Fiero is a big car.

Chevrolet continually denied seeing Fiero as a threat, or even a replacement for Corvette. Fiero, however, has found enormous popularity, and fills the streets of America in a way which Corvette never has – largely owing to its price. But few observers were surprised when the announcement that the turbo V6 Fiero would not now go into production was made. The story was that the power output of the engine was too high for it to be sold to the general public.

Pontiac's award-winning Fiero was GM's first attempt at a mid-engined car since the unlucky Corvair. Perhaps that's why it never got its 300hp aluminum V6.

However, the Fiero did get its V6 powerplant. Mounted sideways behind the driver in the approved European fashion, it is the basic 2.8 Chevrolet V6 which delivers a respectable 140hp at 5200rpm; hardly the same as the twin turbo, but a noticeable improvement over the original four-cylinder. The presence of the V6 means that top speed lifts from 100 to 125 mph, and two seconds are cut from the 0-60 acceleration time.

When it was first announced, specifying the V6 brought an 'aerodynamic' GT body, featuring the droop snoot and rear wing from the Indy car, plus the uprated suspension package which remains optional on the four-cylinder.

Saying the body package is 'aerodynamic' is slightly misleading; its cavernous interior (compared with European sportscars) results in a substantial frontal area. In the wind tunnel, without its optional rear wing, but with rounded nose-cone and extended rocker panels, the base Fiero achieves an enormous Cd figure of 0.40, and drops only as low as 0.37 with the wing in place.

But these questions are now more or less academic; with 1987 volume at a fraction of its target, Pontiac decided to drop Fiero at the end of the 1988 model year, and final orders for the car were accepted during April of 1988.

With plastic body panels on a steel frame, Fiero could change shape each model year easily, quickly and very cheaply. The 1988 GT model (below right) took the rear wing from the Indy car.

INDEX

BELOW 1955 Ford Thunderbird ABOVE 1929 Packard Coupé OVERLEAF 1984 Chevrolet Corvette